EAST YORKSHIRE

WITHIN LIVING MEMORY

EAST YORKSHIRE

WITHIN LIVING MEMORY

Compiled by the East Yorkshire Federation
of Women's Institutes from contributions sent by
Institutes in the County

Published jointly by
Countryside Books, Newbury
and the EYFWI, Beverley

First published 1998
© East Yorkshire Federation of Women's Institutes 1998

COUNTRYSIDE BOOKS
3 Catherine Road
Newbury, Berkshire

ISBN 1 85306 543 9

Front cover photograph showing the beach at Bridlington
in the 1920s supplied by Shirley Franklin, Driffield WI.

Back cover photograph showing land girls on an East
Riding farm supplied by John Harrison, of Bainton.

Produced through MRM Associates Ltd., Reading
Printed by J. W. Arrowsmith Ltd., Bristol

CONTENTS

FOREWORD

The twentieth century has witnessed dramatic changes to almost every aspect of our lives. As we move towards the millennium, it must be difficult for today's young people to imagine a harvest without a combine harvester, or homes without running water. In 1900, anyone reading of "surfing the net", would surely have expected it to refer to the fishing industry.

Even our coast line has changed, indeed, we are powerless to prevent it; and we have also had a temporary change of name – the East Riding of Yorkshire was for 23 years a part of the county of Humberside, regaining its name in 1996.

Much has remained the same, however. The open area of Beverley Westwood, the Holderness plain, and many of our buildings remain as they have done for centuries. It is this mix of the enduring and the varying, the familiar and the different which makes life so wonderful. We are fortunate that people have long memories, and are prepared to share those memories, to produce this fascinating book, which I am sure will be of interest to old and young, in East Yorkshire and beyond.

Ann Blackburn
Federation Chairman

ACKNOWLEDGEMENTS

The East Yorkshire Federation of Women's Institutes wish to thank all the members who have submitted contributions for this book. We are especially grateful to the non-members who have generously shared their memories with us. In particular, we are indebted to Isobel Shepherdson, the co-ordinator of the project; Joan Clarke for her computer keyboard skills; Audrey Race for her general helpfulness; and Joan Drake for the map and chapter headings.

We are also grateful to the staff of Countryside Books whose expert knowledge was always at our disposal and was used with such a delicate touch that we felt publication really was a joint venture.

The photographs from the East Riding of Yorkshire Council, Library and Information Services are acknowledged as they appear in the text.

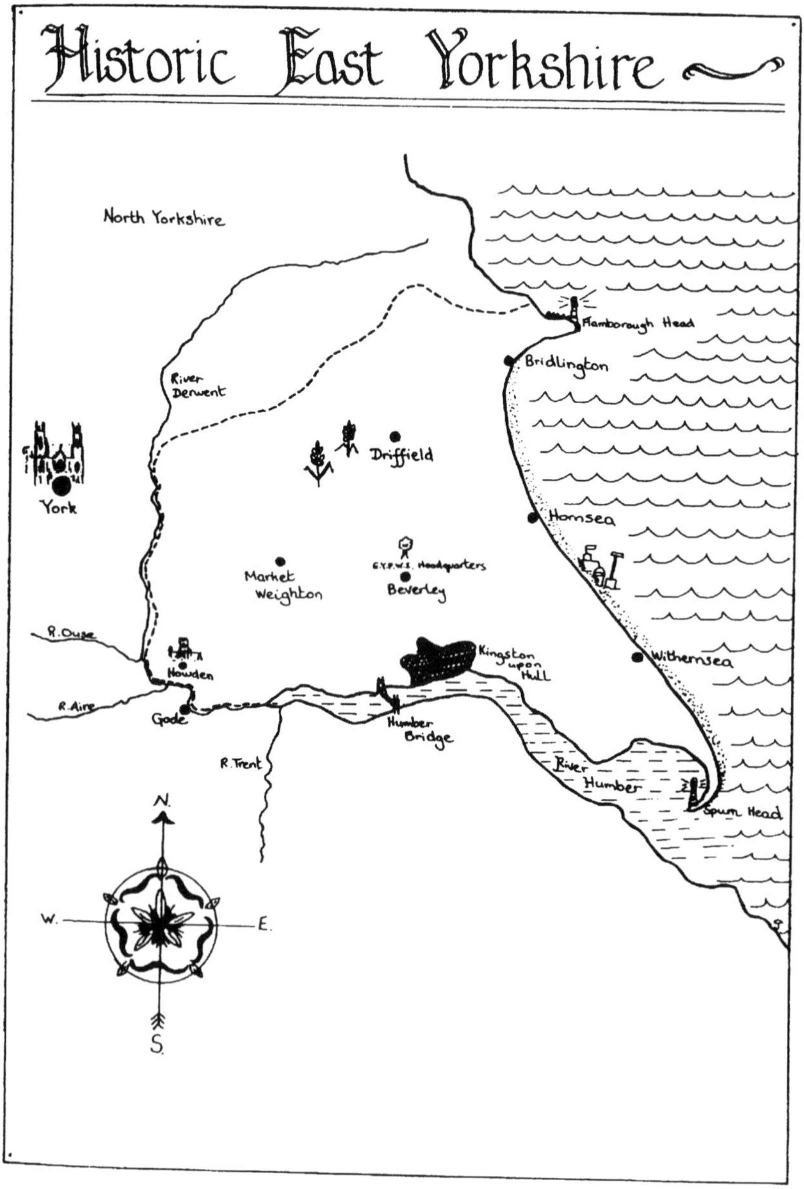

Historic East Yorkshire

North Yorkshire

River Derwent

York

Driffield

Flamborough Head

Bridlington

Hornsea

E.Y.F.W.I. Headquarters

Market Weighton

Beverley

R. Ouse

Howden

R. Aire

Gode

Kingston upon Hull

Humber Bridge

Withernsea

R. Trent

River Humber

Spurn Head

N.

W. — E.

S.

LIST OF CONTRIBUTING INSTITUTES

Contributions have been received from the following
East Yorkshire Women's Institutes

Atwick ● Bainton ● Barmston ● Beeford ● Bempton
Bishop Wilton ● Brandesburton ● Bridlington
Burstwick ● Cottingham ● Cottingham Green
Driffield ● Ellerker ● Elloughton cum Brough
Fangfoss with Bolton ● Hedon ● Hollym
Holme on Spalding Moor ● Hook ● Hornsea
Howden ● Hutton Cranswick ● Kilham ● Leven
Londesborough ● Marshland ● Nafferton
North Ferriby ● Patrington ● Pocklington
Rawcliffe ● Roos ● Rudston ● Seaton Ross
Sewerby ● Snaith ● South Cave ● Stamford Bridge
Sutton on Hull ● Thorngumbald ● Wawne ● Welton
Welton cum Melton ● Willerby & Kirk Ella

TOWN & COUNTRY LIFE

LIFE IN TOWN AND COUNTRY

Life on a country estate, and on a canal barge. Life in a city, and in a small rural village. These snapshots of East Yorkshire give a flavour of what it was like to live in this beautiful area within living memory.

ON A CANAL BARGE

'My father owned the barge named *Chrysoidine*, and traded between Driffield and Hull, carrying 70 tons of corn for E.B. Bradshaw & Sons, Bell Mills, Driffield. There were Father, Mother, my two older sisters and myself on board. I was three weeks old when first taken aboard in the 1930s.

We went down to Hull with an empty barge, taking us approximately one day. We used King George Dock mostly, but occasionally Alexander Dock. We would go to the silo in King George's and await our turn to be loaded. We took on 18 stone bags which Dad stowed in the hold by himself. The bags came down in monkey boxes and Father took them off on his back and stowed them in the hold. When this was achieved we then set off for Driffield. We came through a large lock from the dock into the River Humber, back to the harbour into the River Hull.

The Humber could get very rough at times, especially when we were empty. Mother would always have me up on deck going round the Humber in case of accidents. I used to get very frightened and if it was very rough Mam and I used to go on a tram up to town and meet Dad in the harbour. The River Hull was tidal up to New Lock. There were five locks and four swing bridges to manipulate on the canal. When we got to Driffield, Bradshaws would send a man with a rully to collect the cargo. Father would secure the bags to a chain and my sisters would heave them out on to the rully. This was done until the barge was empty.

In 1936 we took the barge to Thorne to have a Ford engine

Princes Dock, Hull c1900. (East Riding of Yorkshire Council, Library and Information Services)

fitted. Before that we used a square-rigged sail, or if the wind was not in the right quarter Father would move it along with boat hooks. These were poles about 20 feet long with a flattened prong of iron at one end and a round flat piece of wood at the other. Father would plunge the iron end into the river bed and the other end into his shoulder and push the barge along. When we were coming up loaded, Mother would "bow-haul" the barge along. She had a sail-cloth harness round her shoulders attached to a rope on the barge. No mean feat for a woman.

We were in Hull for many of the air raids during the war. If things got very bad when we were in King George Dock we used to go into the basement of the silo to shelter. We used a torch to find some bags to sit on as there were no lights down there. You could hear rats running around. Father always maintained that the Germans would never bomb the silo as it was a landmark for them.

During the war years, my parents had to have special passes to be allowed on the docks. They also had seamen's ration books which allowed them more food than the normal rations. To help out our meals, Father would shoot the odd rabbit or duck. We also ate waterhen's eggs and mushrooms gathered from the fields. Mother did all the cooking and even baked bread on a two-burner Valor paraffin stove with a detachable oven.

Our personal and household washing was kept to be done at home. Our living/sleeping quarters were in the aft cabin. We had a small coal fire in an iron fireplace. We sat on a bench that went around the back of the cabin. A table pulled down for our meals. Father and I sat at the table, whilst Mother and my two sisters balanced their plates on their knees. There were cupboards and drawers behind our seats. Our lighting came from a brass paraffin lamp hanging from the cabin top. There were two or three round deck lights in the deck which let in enough light during daylight hours.

Mam and Dad had a bed in a cupboard at one side of the cabin with double doors to close it off during the day. My bed was on a shelf in a narrower cupboard at the other side of the cabin. Underneath the shelf was where we kept the washing-up bowl etc.

My sisters slept in the foc'stle at the front end of the barge. Our drinking water was kept in a zinc tank on the deck. It used to get warm in the summer. We used to take that on at Riverhead Driffield.

I only attended Driffield school when we were at home, which was about every other week. We were only in Hull about two or three days at a time and not always in the same dock, so there was no point in going to a school there.

Watersports were held annually in Riverhead up to and including 1939 when they were abandoned due to the war. This consisted of various swimming races, hand paddle boat races and greasy pole etc. There were very good prizes to be had – lead crystal, clocks, watches, canteens of cutlery and many more. All this was finished off with an evening open-air dance at Riverhead.

There were only about four keels left using the canal by the early 1940s. Gradually it got down to two. My father sold our keel in September 1944. The other keel made one more journey before the canal was left to go into disrepair.' *(Joan Grainger – Driffield WI)*

▨ Full Sutton Village in 1947 ▨

'In 1947 I arrived at Full Sutton, a 'towny' from Birmingham. I was married to a farmer's son from Youlethorpe. The village was half full of relations and I felt I had arrived in a foreign land as I found the local dialect very difficult to understand at times. Unfortunately that broad dialect is no longer heard.

During the war many acres of land were taken from the farmers and Full Sutton 'drome was built – bombers flew from there to Germany, but in 1947 the planes had gone and the men demobilised and sent on their way home. No houses had been built during this time and accommodation was very difficult to find. The council offered us an empty Nissen hut, but we were offered a small cottage, the middle one in a terrace of three. The rent was the princely sum of 5/- per week.

There was no electricity in the village – that arrived some six or seven years later. Paraffin lamps and candles were used. Cooking was in a fireside oven and hot water ladled from a side boiler – often sooty. A paraffin stove in a stand was used for boiling pans and a small oven stood on top. It worked well and food did not taste of paraffin. One outside tap served the three cottages and the toilet was an earth closet down the bottom of the garden. So chamber pots were a must. Those never did change.

Two buses ran each morning at 8 am – one to York, one to Malton but no buses ran back to the village after 5 pm. Those working in York could only get back to a place over a mile away, and that mile in open country had to be walked every night all year round whatever the weather. My husband at that time worked for a small bus company. During the week he drove a lorry transporting animals and other agricultural crops. At the weekend he drove buses taking parties of people fishing, cricketing etc and to the sea side. I saw very little of him as he worked all hours for a flat rate of £4.10s per week. No days off, no weekends, no holidays.

The village itself was a very quiet place, complete with duck pond – later filled in and concreted over to provide parking for cars. The village green and pond were used, before my time, as a place to rest animals and geese being walked to market in York. They grazed on the green and slaked their thirst at the pond. The farmers knew every gap in every hedge. Today there are more gaps than hedge. There was an old cottage squashed between two others that belonged to a man called Donkey Jack. He took his donkey through the cottage to the back and used the front himself – a windowless hovel with a large wood shelf which was his bed.

The school was at Skirpenbeck and the children from Sutton had to walk, some down the roads, others across fields – almost two miles. My children were taught to ride cycles and had to ride to school whatever the weather.

The cottage adjoining ours was the post office – also the home of the postmistress. The postman cycled for hours every day in all weather delivering mail to outlying farms as well as the village – it must have been a slog. Another man was a council worker – the road man – he kept them clean and gritted in icy weather and had only a cycle to use. We got more gritting done then, we get nothing now with all the modern equipment.

We hadn't lived there long when a use was found for the empty Nissen huts. DPs (displaced persons), people who had lost everything in their own countries through the war and Nazi occupation, were brought over and housed in the old RAF camp. They queued every week at the post office for the allowance given to them. The buses were always packed with them and I remember the overpowering smell of the garlic that they used in their food.

The buses then were so packed it's a wonder the bottoms didn't fall out. The DPs eventually were dispersed to various parts of the country – and then the planes came back. This time with the Americans. Dreadful, noisy, screaming jets that terrified small children and animals. Screaming and swooping round the sky and one could not hear the radio through the noise. The radio had two batteries and one was collected each week and charged up for 6d. The batteries were nearly as big as the radio.

By this time we had a small farm and one day my husband was ploughing a field and noticed a plane landing – but it wasn't going to reach the air strip. He watched in horror as it appeared to be heading straight for him and didn't know whether to stay on the tractor or get off and run. It so happened that a freight train – the Beeching Axe was yet to fall – full of fish from Hull was chugging along and the plane crashed into the train. There was fish everywhere. The two men in the plane were taken to hospital, injured but not fatally.

Eventually the planes and the Americans left and then came the rockets. Three rockets were installed and when emergency practice was in operation we could see the huge hangars rolled back off these giants and the rockets were raised to point to the skies, tall, slim , white and menacing. Thank God they never had to be used. People in the villages round about did not feel safe as the rockets themselves would have been targeted from afar.

During the years we lived there most of our food was delivered. An order was given to a traveller on Mondays and the goods were delivered on Tuesdays. Vans selling bread, meat, fish, hardware all came round. We travelled to Pocklington for 6d or to York for 9d and those buses were packed. There were very few cars and we all walked miles to get to our destinations. If anyone was ill, the doctor called and then sent the medicines through on the local bus. Can you imagine that happening now?

In 1963 there was a meeting in the village reading room when men from London and the local council and villagers discussed building the prison on the 'drome. The land was government property and so of course they had their own way and about 20 years later the prison was built.' *(M. Allison – Stamford Bridge WI)*

▣ GROWING UP IN HULL ▣

'My memories of Hull begin about 1930 when I started school in Bean Street off Anlaby Road in Hull. Kingston upon Hull to give it its full name.

Hedon, looking down from the church tower early in the century.
(East Riding of Yorkshire Council, Library and Information Services)

The school was called the Sir Henry Cooper School. This was to be the first of five schools by the time I reached 14 years of age. We had lived in Linnaeus Street for a few years, moving away when I was 10 or 11.

We could walk through Vauxhall Grove and on to Hessle Road. Most of the shopping was done there and we used to go to Mr Sandlands for a 6d fry, that is liver, kidney and sausage, maybe even a chop included. There was a shop that only sold eggs at 1/- a dozen and like the baker's dozen we got 13. Shops did not sell everything as they do today. The chemist was a real chemist, no pots or pans or photo frames to be had there.

Soap was bought at the ironmonger's, not the grocer's. No scented soap for us, it was either Carbolic or Premier. The Atora Suet people had a large covered wagon pulled by two oxen, which was a rare sight as it came along Anlaby Road. My mother bought her suet from the butcher's, a big piece cost 2d. She shredded as much as was needed then kept the remainder in the bag of flour, ready for next time.

Market Weighton High Street c1921 – still safe to stand in the street! (East Riding of Yorkshire Council, Library and Information Services)

Although times were hard when there was no work, I do not remember ever going hungry, but I'm glad I wasn't a parent at that time. We often had to have a grocery voucher for the week. This was spent at Wm. Jackson's on the corner of Bean Street. No free milk from the milkman, it had to be evaporated milk in a tin. It was this same shop where I could go just before closing time on a Saturday for 2d of bacon pieces and a large tin of tomatoes. These, with hot bread cakes which my mother had got up very early to make, made us a very special Sunday breakfast. The Public Benefit shoe shop was where we had to go to exchange a voucher for black boots for the boys and black lace-up shoes for me. At school we were given a green ticket, a little bit like blotting paper with black printing on it, to exchange for our dinner at the Day Street dinner rooms (which always smelled of mushy peas). We sat on forms at long trestle tables.

When my Dad was out of work in the winter, it was good when there was a decent fall of snow. He, along with many others, would go down to the Labour Exchange with his shovel to sign on to clear the snow from the roads. They had to be there very early. When he came home he would then go to the big houses on Anlaby Road and knock on a door and say, "Please Missus, can I clear your front for 3d?" If he only got four to do it was a shilling and well worth having.

Salvation Army Sunday school was a must on Sunday and one night during the week. In the winter time we could have a cup of cocoa or a saucer of mushy peas at the night session. Sunday nights in the summer we could go for a walk and if we were lucky we might have a penny to share. This we used for 1d of bottle bottoms, which were broken boiled sweets. I don't remember any arguments about who got the most.

The milkman came with a pony and trap, the milk being in an oval metal container. He used either a one pint or half pint measure to serve the milk, which was poured into our jug or basin. We also had a fruit and veg man come round with a horse and cart. It was like a market stall on wheels. My memories of the coal man are of him shouting, "Coal, 1/9d a bag". I seem to remember they were ten-stone bags in Hull when other areas were eight-stone. Then, of course, there was the rag and bone man, who gave us a halfpenny for a jam jar. I think our rags were turned into clipped rugs.

Life wasn't all doom and gloom. It did have its lighter times. West Park was along Anlaby Road, and we often went there for a few hours. One day six of us went together. My mother must have had to go somewhere where she could not take the two youngest boys, so I was entrusted to take care of them for the day. We had sandwiches packed up and I was given 6d to share among us through the day. The first penny went on a pennyworth of 'gammy' fruit: bruised apples, over ripe bananas, squashy oranges and the like. We got a big bag full. When we were in the park we got two halfpenny ice cream sandwiches, breaking each one in half for four of us. We considered the two in the pram were too young for ice cream sandwiches! Well, we had to make that 6d last all day! The pram was a big brown Marmet my Mam had bought secondhand for 5/-. It had three loose seats with a well underneath so one could sit either end

Cottingham's main village street c1900. (Eileen Green – Cottingham WI)

with feet down in the well.

We had a lovely day and were on our way home when, suddenly, we came to a halt. We had run into some plant pots that were on the pavement in front of the ironmonger's shop, probably Mallorys. A woman rushed out to us wanting our name and address and we were told a policeman would be coming to the house. I told the lads not to say anything when we got home. We lived in fear of that policeman who never came.

Thinking of policemen reminds me of the blue box on the corner of Argyle Street, just like the Dr Who box!' *(Ruth Walker – Bishop Wilton WI)*

❖ VILLAGE LIFE IN WELTON ❖

'Welton village must surely be one of the most attractive in the East Riding. It is fairly quiet now, but in days gone by it was a busy thriving community. Like all villages it has its personalities. Ralph Widd was one of Welton's best known and respected residents. Ralph was born in 1910 and before he died he recorded some of his memories of village life for South Hunsley School:

I have lived all my life in the village of Welton. The most outstanding change is the growth of the village, with new houses and bungalows being built by people coming out of the town to live in the country.

When I was a lad, living here was typical of village life. We were always a village community. We couldn't go very far away, as in my early days there wasn't any buses and we had to make our own entertainment. When it was necessary to go into Hull we had to walk to either Brough or Ferriby railway station to get the train into Hull, and to walk back from Brough or Ferriby on our return.

There were roads into Hull, but they were made of very rough ironstone mainly. Transport was horse and cart or ponies and traps. Farmers from around the district would set off from home at 2 am with their horses and rullies (waggons) to go to the market to sell their produce in Hull (potatoes, vegetables, eggs etc). Everything they had to sell they took to the market.

With the advent of motorised transport, I think that on the

Hutton Cranswick's Forester's Hall and the Packhorse Inn. (East Riding of Yorkshire Council, Library and Information Services)

whole it was welcomed by the villagers because it meant that they could get away into Hull a bit more than they used to do. When buses first started they were "charabancs" which were open topped. They used to pull a hood over when it rained.

The first motor car in the village, I think, belonged to the Squire. It had wooden wheels as far as I can remember, but I don't recall what make the car was. The Squire was not really the old traditional stoic squire, and I remember two Squires, Admiral Harrison Broadley, then Captain Harrison Broadley who took over when I was young. The young Squire was a very smart chap, immaculately dressed when he used to come riding to the hounds meetings that were held in the village twice a year. They met at Welton House and came down through the village. All the villagers had to salute him or say "good morning" to him.

He was also a very good all-round sportsman. He was a wonderful shot when we used to go bush beating. He was one of the shots who could get the first of the covey of partridges and the last. You don't see many men today who can do that.

Entertainment for us children was usually held at the Estate Hall, which was built by the Squire, and we used to have concerts, parties, with whist drives for the older people, and for the men of the village there was the billiard hall and card rooms attached to the Estate Hall. The men in the village played a lot of cards in those days.

Self-made entertainment was mainly football and cricket on the village green, and at night we used to play a game called "Foxes". One person would be picked as the Fox, and run away and hide, other chaps were called the Hounds, and would set off and try and find the Fox. We used to have some real good fun. One year one of the Foxes got up a fir tree just outside the Estate Hall, and not knowing, the local policeman (who used to always parade around the village, moving us on if we stood in groups outside shops), he found this lad up the tree, and told him to come down. The lad didn't realise that it was the policeman, and gave him a lot of cheek, hence the Sergeant slapped him across the backside with his stick when the lad came down.

The church in those days played a big part in village life. If you could sing at all when you were a boy, you got into the choir, because the headmaster, Mr Boardman was a very highly trained musician. We always had a full choir of boys, men and a few ladies. The Squire and all his family used to come down to the Sunday morning services and sit in their special pews, and the church was mainly full. There is also another little church on the estate at Waudby Manor. The choir used to go there once a month. We had to walk through Welton Dale, which was a beautiful walk, have the service, and then walk back again with the vicar, Rev Blackwall. We all looked up to the vicar as one of the leading men of the village, and we always respected him very much.

There was a large general store in the village called Francis Myers. They used to deliver all the groceries, etc. round all the villages by horse and cart. We had three small sweet shops, two public houses, a post office, two blacksmiths, a butcher, a tailor – which later became a cobbler's shop – a police station with cells for prisoners, and a flour mill which was driven by water from the springs in the dale. We had two chapels, a Primitive and Wesleyan chapel. We also had Welton Dale Society and the Druids. We used to pay 1d a week into their funds in case we became ill at any time, and were then able to draw a little bit of money out, to help towards paying any doctor's bills.

The churches got together and arranged outings in my early days, to East Park in Hull, and later on they arranged an outing to Bridlington once a year. The tradesmen of the village used to lend us vans and lorries and Mr Myers, head of the general stores, used to do most of the "arranging". It was a very great day for all the villagers and there were quite a lot of lorries and vans to take us.

With regards to employment in the village, there wasn't a lot more than working on the estate or working for Myers. There were one or two odd placements, such as the undertakers in the village, or the coalman – where probably one lad might get a job for so long. In holiday times we used to go potato picking, ket lop pulling, walking to Brough and golf caddying, anything to help the budget at home. There wasn't a lot more until Blackburn aircraft factory opened in later years, and that gave more scope for boys in apprenticeships.

Christmas in the village was a very big occasion. We used to go carol singing or Christmas singing in those days, on Christmas Day or Boxing Day to the big houses round the village, and they always gave us either an orange or a mince pie or 3d. At the Squire's house we all got 6d *and* an orange and by jove, that was a lot of money in those days. We thought it was marvellous. We were well received in all the big houses, no one refused to give us anything.' *(Hazel Widd – Welton WI)*

◫ On the Londesborough Estate ◫

'Sonny Harrison was born at Warrendale Farm, part of the Londesborough Estate that lies on the southern tip of the Yorkshire Wolds. His grandfather and father had worked the farm for two generations. Most of the people in Londesborough village, which nestles among the folding hills that run down towards Market Weighton, worked on the estate. There were cartmen, woodmen, gardeners, joiners, and surprisingly, an electrician, as well as a number of women who did domestic work at the large house known as Londesborough Park.

When Sonny was a boy in the late 1920s, "Everybody knew everybody and nothing ever seemed to change very much at all." There were only four cars in the village – Mr and Mrs Booth who lived at Londesborough Park, and owned the estate, had two, the estate agent had one, and one belonged to the parson, the Rev Cave-Browne-Cave. Sonny's family went about in a horse-drawn trap with candle-lit lanterns for headlamps. In the winter there was a sledge, with a parcel place at the back. Sonny loved it when the snow came. The sledge would swing around corners at a pace, throwing parcels flying from their rack, and people from their places on the back seat.

In the old stables, which have now been converted into a comfortable group of dwelling houses around a cobbled courtyard, was an old Mercedes. It was built like a farm wagon with an open top, paraffin head-lamps, and a magnifying lamp

Eastgate, Driffield, and a peaceful spot for children's games. (East Riding of Yorkshire Council, Library and Information Services)

in the front. In its day it had been used on shooting expeditions – to take picnics to shooters out on the farms with good roads. It was in use up to about 1923, but Sonny had never seen it going. It stood there for years and the village children used to lark about in it. Mr and Mrs Booth had a Lanchester driven by a French chauffeur, a Monsieur Delaval.

Londesborough was well known for its shooting. Near Warrendale Farm was a spot called the ice-house. It was a great hole in the ground. In winter ice was mixed with straw and put in the cavity to make a cold-store for pheasant and an assortment of perishable game. The food kept fresh well into the spring – May, or even early June. The mound marking the ice-house can still be seen today.

The village had its own water and electricity supplies. The electricity was generated by a steam engine housed in the woodyard. The engine provided electricity for All Saints church and the Reading Room, and a big cable ran down Low Street to Londesborough Park where the power was fed into two enormous banks of accumulators. The engine was switched off at 10 pm and the lights at the Hall would gradually go down and down as the power diminished. Then the electrician would be called for, to throw the switches over to the power stored by the batteries and the lights would grow bright again. The villagers used oil lamps and candles. In later years the generator was run by a Crossley diesel engine. National grid electricity and mains water came to Londesborough in 1948.

One of the characters of the village was a retired keeper called Toby Consett: a somewhat rotund, Victorian man who liked his nip of rum. On one occasion the founder of the Boy Scout movement, Sir Baden Powell, was invited to Londesborough Park for the shooting season. Toby was given the duty of look-out. He had to watch for Baden Powell's motor car as it came into view on the road above the village. As soon as he saw it, Toby was to fire two gunshots. These were to be picked up by another keeper, who in turn would make a signal to the house that the eminent visitor had arrived.

"How will I know the car?" Toby asked about nervously, afraid he might get it wrong.

"It'll be flying a flag Toby," came the sardonic reply.

There weren't many cars about on the roads, and no doubt Baden Powell's would be easily recognisable, especially in relation to a horse and cart. The Park kept twelve to 20 servants before 1939, but the old way of life petered out with the onset of the Second World War.

There are lots of stories about Toby. Dr Ashwin, the present owner of Londesborough Estate, remembers how, one Monday morning, Mrs Peacock and Sonny's Aunt Lil were troubled that Toby hadn't been seen of late. He wasn't at church on Sunday, and now he wasn't around on Monday either. They got the clerk and the trustees to open up his little house. And there he was, flat in the bed as if he'd flown this world. Thinking him dead the two women began to bemoan his end.

"Ah, 'e's gone this time Lil," said Mrs Peacock.

"Aye," replied Lil, "an' 'e was a nice ol' man too, and now 'e's dead."

With that the supposed corpse sat bolt upright in the bed with a loud cry.

"Nay, I'm not dead yet. I'm not. And I'll thank thee to get out. Get out of my 'ouse this minute."

There was no thieving in the village. After harvest, hen-houses would be carted off to the shorn fields where the chickens would feed on the gleanings. At night someone would go and fasten them in to keep them safe from foxes. Next day the huts would be opened again, and the chickens would roam free. They were never stolen.

Everybody went up to Warrendale Farm. Quite a few of the lads and men had motor-bikes. Sonny warmed to the memory of old names like Triumph, Douglas Scott, Royal Enfield, Raleigh. There was a Coventry Eagle bought at the great cost of 7/6d, and a Harley-Davidson motor-bike and side-car. Nobody had licences, and no one seemed to know where all the bikes came from. But these things didn't matter one jot, for they all had a grand time riding around the farm paddock and the stubble fields after harvest.

There was a close community spirit. Along with the Atkinsons and the Hewitsons, the Harrisons just about kept the village school going with children. "You could hear the blacksmith's anvil ringing when you came home from school," he recalled, warmly remembering childhood pleasures, "and you'd stop to watch him shoeing the horses. The blacksmith went when the horses went, when the tractors took over."

Nobody trusted the new-fangled tractors at first.

"Tractors are no good," the local farmers said. "They'll never work. They puddle the soil."

They said much the same about other innovations.

"Combines!" they snorted, "they'll not take on in this country. They might well work in America, but not here."

But the tractors and combines took over. Altered everything, even the rhythm of the seasons. They brought harvest forward to July.

When the war was over, people went off working on the land. The wages were always poor and you couldn't get the labour.

Sonny's family were contented enough: they had plenty of everything they needed, and expectations were less than they are now. But by and large they were poor old days. There was a lot of poverty. It was cold in the winter and there were no washing machines. It was hard work, and as Sonny was quick to remind me: "People wouldn't stand for it now."' *(Audrey Dunne – Londesborough WI)*

▣ SNOW AND FLOOD: 1947 & 1953 ▣

'The severe winter of 1947 was felt countrywide, but there were two local items of some interest.

One was that a steam train got lost in snow drifts for four days, between Market Weighton and Beverley. The other was that the Kiplingcotes Derby, the oldest flat race in the country (pre-dating

Floods in Driffield's Exchange Street in 1910. (East Riding of Yorkshire Council, Library and Information Services)

the Derby at Epsom) and which has been run every year since 1519, was carried out by a lone farmer in 1947, to maintain the tradition. The race usually takes 30 to 40 minutes but in 1947, with the severe conditions, it took four and a half hours to complete.' *(Eric Longbottom, of Cottingham)*

'The great snowstorms of January and February 1947 were dreadful. Villages were cut off, roads buried under ten foot drifts, and trains buried. Because of rationing most people had no stocks of food. Water was frozen, coal could not get through. The *Leeds Mercury* of Monday 10th February said: "Men of the RAF Mountain Rescue Service from Topcliffe, and a team of Army bulldozer drivers from Ripon took nearly 600lbs of food, bread, margarine, tinned meat and fruit and flour to help the village of Huggate. They were guided in the dark from Warter by compass and radio." The bulldozers were stopped at Minningdale Farm by the height of the drifts. The RAF men each carried 50lb packs on their backs. Wearing snow-shoes and hooded dufflecoats, they struggled through breast-high snow to relieve the little village which had been cut off for a week and had little food or fuel left.

There was five feet of snow in the main street. Houses were partly buried and had tunnels dug out to their doors. The local men had tried to dig themselves out of the village but had only managed 100 feet in one day, and the wind blew much of the loose snow back again. The servicemen managed to get through and then struggled back to Warter in a state of exhaustion. A few days later the bulldozers managed to break through the drifts to clear a narrow way.' *(Ella Musgrove for Fangfoss with Bolton WI)*

'I honestly cannot recall the bad winter of 1946/7 – somewhere there is a picture of me in a pixie-hood and knitted suit with leggings, helping to sweep snow in my grandmother's garden. What I can remember however, is the aftermath – as the snow thawed, the flood waters came.

I was almost five years old, living with my parents and sister – my brother was away at school. We had two steps up to the front door of our house, and my father assured us that the water would not rise above them. Two days later the water level was half way up the dining room table legs!

In my grandmother's house, the water rose a lot higher, so she and my aunts moved in with us. We put the larger items of furniture on trestles and tables and all eight of us, plus the dog and smaller items of furniture, moved upstairs for a few weeks. Fortunately it was a large house with fireplaces in some of the bedrooms. The cooking was done mostly on the fire in my parents' bedroom, which suited me fine, as I was also sleeping in there on a camp bed. My youngest aunt was sharing my bedroom with floor-to-ceiling furniture from downstairs. When she wanted to go to bed all she had to do was squeeze round the door, climb over the bottom of the bed, walk up it and snuggle down! As far as I can recall, nothing fell on her in the night, and she is still around at 86 to tell the tale.

Bread and milk were delivered by boat, and placed in baskets lowered from the upstairs windows. In fact, food was sent to all the flooded areas of Britain from as far away as Australia and Canada, and large amounts of tinned food were shared out as the floods subsided.

There was a rise in the land just behind our house, and at regular intervals my father took me on his back and the dog in his arms, and we had a little exercise on our postage stamp of land. Our little terrier slept on a hearth rug at the top of the stairs, and never put a paw wrong all the time we lived up there.

Of course the water did eventually subside. The coal was retrieved from the farthest corners of the house, the foundations were pumped dry and the dining room table still bore the water marks when we gave it away in 1969!

As an adult, I can now realise how awful it must have been, but at the time, to one small girl, it was a great adventure.' *(Jen Cochrane – Wawne WI)*

'I suppose that it was not the usual childhood. From the age of three I lived at the end of a windswept sand-spit in a small community that was rarely as many as 30 in population. Our reason for being there was the Humber lifeboat which was located at Spurn Head. My father moved there to be second coxswain, later to become coxswain when my grandfather retired (a time which I nearly never saw).

The year was 1953 and I had recently started school. The eventful day had begun quite normally. However, in the late morning I noticed an anxious look appear on my parents' faces as they listened to the weather forecast on the wireless. We were warned not to go out of the house. A hurricane was threatening the Humber area.

Storm boards were fixed to protect the windows. Our houses were only yards from the sea. For a child it was exciting to hear the increasing roar from the sea.

Later that afternoon the phone rang. It was what had been dreaded. A ship was in distress and the lifeboat was launched to go to the rescue.

My two elder brothers and I noticed that the sea was coming under the outer porch door and forming a very enticing venue for sailing our toy boats. This we decided was great fun. My mother missed us and the timeless nature of a good time, special to childhood, was cut short by a command to return inside the cottage proper. For some unknown reason, we will never know why, I was unobserved and stayed playing in my private ocean.

The rescue accomplished, the lifeboat returned to the station. When my father returned home he looked around and asked where was the little one? With a gasp of horror, my mother realised that I must be playing in the porch. Unceremoniously, I was grabbed and pulled inside in less than a millisecond. Like most children, when their parents feel guilty and relieved, I was in big trouble! It was not as big as it might have been.

Approximately two minutes later (I do not exaggerate), the porch door was broken by the power of the sea, which swept into where I had been playing. Without doubt I would have been dragged out to sea and certain death. Newspapers would have reported the tragic death of a five year old in the East Coast floods.' *(Joe Buchan, of Hornsea)*

CHURCH & CHAPEL

Sunday was a day of rest, when children were expected to attend Sunday school and most families went at least once to church or chapel. Sunday school anniversaries and outings were high spots of the year for children who had few other organised treats.

⊞ THE CHURCH IN THE STACKYARD ⊞

The hamlet of Cowlam, on the Bridlington to Sledmere road, consists of four farms, a church, a vicarage, the foreman's house, three cottages, four council houses and a bungalow. In the 1920s Cowlam Manor was owned by a London finance company called Kerrs & Herricks, who had a manager living in the

The whole village would have turned out for the vicar's daughter's wedding at Rudston in 1913. (East Riding of Yorkshire Council, Library and Information Services)

farmhouse. At harvest there would be up to 40 men living on the farm. There were two huge farmhouse kitchens where the men had their meals, with the bell over the back door like a school bell to summon them for their food.

The church is built of the same oblong blocks of stone as Bempton church. It has no side aisles, the belfry is an open alcove with a seat across, just enough for one person to sit on, and there is no tower, the bell being in the open. Until 1928 there was a resident rector, the Revd James Oliver, who had lived there since 1891. He was very popular. The hired men were away from their homes for a year at a time, with only occasional visits. He acted as counsellor to them, with regular church services, and mingled with them during the week.

In 1928 Mr John Sawden bought Cowlam. He split the original one farm into four and reorganised the estate, and renovated the church. Every Sunday afternoon, without fail, services were held there by the Revd Sparrow from Luttons Ambo. The church played a large part in our lives. Every Sunday we donned our best clothes and went to the service. Out of a population of about 36, we had a regular gathering of 15 to 20 people.

My sister and I also often played the organ for services. Sometimes when I was practising in the summer evenings or on Sunday morning the men from the farms would come into church and sing their hearts out. An old uncle who used to come in summer to do odd jobs and harvest would say, "Come and play some hymns for us, Kaffy". He loved it and the men would usually join us when they heard the organ. My sister cleaned the church, and woe betide anyone who brought any dirt in!

The farmers' wives from the surrounding farms came to church whenever possible, walking for two miles. It was the only time they got out, before they had cars. Sometimes their husbands would bring them in the pony and trap – but not often! After church the vicar encouraged his congregation to linger and talk to each other. It was a good meeting place, the ladies catching up on the happenings of the week. My mother often walked as far as Top Cowlam with them for the companionship.

The Harvest Festival was the highlight of the year. We

decorated every part of the church and the farm men brought in ladders to put ropes across to hold the paraffin lamps – it was the only evening service of the year. The church was always full. It was a lovely setting, with the stackyards, stables and farm buildings around us.

Children were always very welcome at the services; there being no Sunday school they all came to church. They were mostly very good – wriggling but not disruptive! They were given their prizes every year, and in the summer we all went along with the congregation and Sunday school from Lutton church and Primitive Methodist chapel to Scarborough. It was a much looked forward to day out. All the children were given sixpence each – it's surprising what you could buy for sixpence! We thought we were rich. Our usual pocket money was a penny.

We left Cowlam in 1943. Soon after the war electricity was installed in the hamlet. The powers-that-be in York told the local people that if they wanted to continue having services in the church they must keep it in repair themselves. So when the farmers were out at market etc they asked around for tools and implements. After a great deal of effort they were able to hold a sale at Top Farm of farm machinery and tools. An auctioneer from Driffield gave his time free and sold everything, which raised a good sum. The churchwardens and council then paid to install electricity in the church, and had it redecorated. Today the living is joined with Sledmere and there is a service once a month on a Sunday afternoon – and they still have a full church for Harvest Festival.' *(Joyce Mumby – Bempton WI)*

▣ MUSICAL HOOK ▣

'These days it is often said that we don't have any characters, but in days past at Hook there were one or two who attended church. We had in the congregation the village blacksmith and a local nurseryman. The first was a baritone and the second a tenor, and they were very good musicians but used to compete with each other. The results were quite amusing. One day the tenor got so carried away that he started to sing another verse of a hymn after

The ancient church at Hook, attended by generations of village people.
(Bessie Clarkson – Hook WI)

everyone had finished. The vicar of that time was not very pleased.

The young organist used to cycle to church twice on Sundays (as most churches had two services a day then) from Sykehouse, a village about twelve miles from here. When I say his fee for the year was only £5, he certainly deserved it.' *(Bessie Clarkson – Hook WI)*

◙ A Pennyworth of Sweets ◙

'I was born at East End Farm, Kilham in 1948 and christened in All Saints church by Mr Crankshaw, the vicar at the time. He lived in the old vicarage behind Kilham school. On Mother's Day he let those of us who went to Sunday school go into his garden and pick violets, snowdrops etc to make into little posies for our mothers. I went to Sunday school from five years of age, with my friend.

My mother used to give me twopence for the collection at Sunday school, which was at two in the afternoon, so we would call at the shop near the church and get a pennyworth of sweets. Jackflaps, or maybe a gobstopper or two, and then we went to church. We sat three rows from the front on the side where the pulpit was. Right near the radiator was a loose plank of wood, so while praying we would have a goody or two and the paper was passed to whoever was at that end of the pew. They would lift up this loose bit of wood and pop the paper in. It got a bit full sometimes.' *(Ruth Dennis – Kilham WI)*

◨ SUNDAY SCHOOL ANNIVERSARIES ◨

'The Primitive Methodist Sunday school anniversary at Kilham was always celebrated on the last Sunday in May. The large building faced up Driffield Road. Miss Alice Turnbull (later Mrs Parker) trained the youngsters for singing. There were three services on a Sunday and one on the Monday evening. All the scholars had the Monday afternoon holiday from the village school. All the Sunday school teachers and scholars supported each other's anniversaries, Primitives, Wesleyans and the Anglicans.

At the Kilham Sunday school anniversary in the late 1920s. (Ada Coates – Kilham WI)

Fund raisers for the Primitive Methodist chapel fund touring Kilham village in the 1930s. (Margaret Parker – Kilham WI)

Wesleyan Sunday school anniversary was always celebrated on the first Sunday in June and the school scholars also had the Monday afternoon as holiday prior to the Monday evening service.

Mr Ashmore who had a General Stores in the village, and Mr Banks who was a joiner and the chapel's organist, trained the children for their singing and recitations. The hymns were printed on a leaflet and sold to the congregation for 2d a sheet. The chapel was crammed full for the services, and many ex-residents of Kilham came back for the anniversary.

On the Monday afternoon holiday the Sunday school scholars sang their anniversary hymns through the village of Kilham. They started at the village pond down East Street. Mr Banks had a small folding harmonium and a boy carried a chair, and the children stopped and sang at various places through the village. They continued up West End, and at Pasture Farm the infants could walk back across the pasture to the Sunday school building in Middle Street, nearly opposite the Bay Horse. The older children had to carry on up to West End Farm before they could finish.

Kilham's Sunday school anniversary programme in 1936. (Ada Coates
– Kilham WI)

The children were ready for their tea at the Sunday school, but Mrs Richard Wilson (from the Grange), wearing a white apron, wouldn't let the children in until it was "time". They ate downstairs, off the green pots with the Kilham Wesleyan Church logo on.

Upstairs the long trestles were set out for the public tea – 1s 6d each! They had the white Kilham Wesleyan china. Beautiful white damask cloths were laid and platefuls of ham and tongue, heaped plates of bread and butter, and jam tarts, buns, cakes and curd cheesecakes. One lady took her silver tea pot and various cakes on individual cake stands, with white crocheted doilies hanging down. There were sometimes two sittings of the public tea. Mr Richard Wilson carved the ham (all home cooked).

The ladies of the church spent all day preparing the tea and Mrs Richard Wilson and Mrs Harry Hoggard, Mrs Charles Middlewood and Mrs Ashmore, and Mrs Tom Wilson and Mrs Croft from Creyke Farm paired up to supervise their tables, assisted by Miss Jeffels, later Mrs George Robson.

After tea everyone went down to the evening's anniversary service. There was a chairman, and a speaker as well as the children's performances.

On the Wednesday evening the children had races in Mr Robson's field, where the bungalow "Trebla Nook" now stands. I remember winning a needlebox full of needles. All the children were given an orange each by Mr Ashmore.

The parish church Sunday school anniversary took place on the first Sunday in July. Children took bunches of flowers and baskets of eggs to "The Egg and Flower" service. These gifts were taken to the cottage hospital in Driffield. When that hospital was "done away with", the gifts went to elderly people who lived in "The Workhouse" which had become an old people's home.' *(Ada Coates – Kilham WI)*

▨ REMEMBERED WITH JOY ▨

'Two village days stand out in my memory. The first was Dedication Day, when we all went to church in the morning and then had the rest of the day off from school to enjoy the Garden Party held in the rectory grounds. A scheme ran through the year for your mother to buy stamps to spend at this wonderful event, with a treasure hunt, coconut shies, hoopla, china stalls, gifts, games and the like. But the highlight of the day was the Tea, free if you went to the Sunday school (we were very smug on the day) – egg and potted meat sandwiches, lettuce (which you would not have eaten at home), cakes and buns and a cup of tea. It was a day remembered with joy for the rest of the year.

The other day, the Sunday school outing, could be your only day out in the year. A coach ride to Hull to the ferry, a paddleboat trip across the Humber, and a short walk to the train to be transported to the glories of Cleethorpes – and all that to look forward to on the way home as well.' (M. Winter – Roos WI)

▨ DRIFFIELD TRIP DAY ▨

'Driffield Trip Day was always held on a Wednesday in August – the Wednesday when the tide was out, during the day at Bridlington. Wednesday was half day closing in Driffield, and on Trip Day it was like a ghost town. The previous Friday evening all the children went to their Sunday school and were given 6d and a ticket for the train. Those who didn't go to Sunday school weren't left out. They had to take a piece of paper with their name on, to a certain place, to qualify.

My brother and I were regular attenders at George Street Methodist chapel so off we went to collect our 6d and a ticket. On the Tuesday evening Mother made mounds of sandwiches. I don't think she enjoyed the trip and there were warnings of, "If you don't behave, we shall not go". We were so excited. Wednesday saw streams of mothers and children going to the station where two trains between 8.30 and 9 am were to take us to Bridlington. The adults purchased their 1/6d tickets from a table in the station yard.

On arrival, the first port of call was Woolworths, an Aladdin's cave, where everything cost 6d. I remember buying a paper parasol and my brother bought a cricket bat. Then to the beach, taken over by Driffielders. Sandwiches, mixed with sand, were eaten and mothers were able to purchase jugs of tea from kiosks on the prom.

It always seemed to rain at some time in the day and suddenly there would be a mass exodus to the shelters, and then gradually people would start to drift back to the sands, only to repeat the whole exercise a little later. Then it would be time to go home.

At Driffield it was usual for all passengers to leave the station through small wicket gates, but because of the vast throng all wanting to leave at once, a large gate, which was locked for 364 days a year, was opened to allow the tired throng to proceed into Riverhead. We were all kept there, until both trains arrived from Bridlington. Then the crossing gates were opened, and preceded by the Driffield Town Silver Band we all marched home.

Trip Day is still carried on in Driffield, but uses a fleet of buses. Not half the fun of pre-war trips.' *(Ursula Theakston – Driffield WI)*

◈ WHITSUN IN GOOLE ◈

'I was born in 1939 and as was tradition in our family, I went to Sunday school. I attended the one attached to St Paul's church in Goole, which has since been demolished. My most vivid memory is the yearly Whitsuntide parades involving all the churches in Goole. All the children attending Sunday school took part.

Different children were given the chance of being on the float, which was on a lorry usually borrowed from Fisons Fertilisers because my father worked there. I remember being on two floats, the one in 1948 more so because I have a photograph to boost the memories. This depicted the children from countries throughout the world, which had been our theme at Sunday school that year. I was a Hawaiian girl. I remember cocoa being mixed and put on my skin to make it brown, and would you believe it, it rained and I ended up striped. I also had to stand all the way with one arm in the air, which was very tiring.

The parade travelled quite some distance around the streets of Goole, ending by the banks of the river for an open air service. It

On the float at Goole's Whit parade in 1948. (M. Bonser – Snaith WI)

was quite hair-raising standing on even a slow moving lorry, when it braked it was difficult keeping one's balance. We had a lot of fun finding materials for clothing and decorations because of the post-war shortages but always managed to put on a good show. Almost all the children of Goole must have been in the parade. I remember looking back from the lorry and it stretched for a very long way and disappeared round a corner. It was of course led by a band.

Some years our feet would stick to the tarmac surface of the road it was so hot. Our church always had a party afterwards, prepared by parents, plus entertainment by any church members young or old. The excitement surrounding this event was quite something. It is surprising that so much could be achieved at a time when we were still suffering shortages as a result of the war.

We were all bought new clothes for Whitsun and I could never understand why they could not be worn until Whit Sunday. Most of my clothes were bought at the Bon Marche store in Goole, run by two very stern ladies dressed in black who did not like children. I used to dread going into their shop. What used to fascinate me was, they would switch on a very dim light bulb as one entered the shop and if one wanted to look at something in a different part this would be switched off and another turned on. I was sorely tempted to walk back and forth to see what they would do but was too terrified of the possible consequences.

When I look back, what wonderful times they were, everyone from children to parents, clergy, churchwardens and Sunday school teachers all taking part and the whole town involved or turning out to watch and join in the service.' *(M.C. Bonser – Snaith WI)*

GETTING ABOUT

It is not so long since we used real horse-power to get about, or relied on a bicycle or our own feet. Memory takes us back to when cars were a rare sight on our roads, and when ferries and steam trains were regular transport.

▧ TRAINS, BUSES AND CARS ▧

'The railways played a large part in our early lives. Fangfoss station was a hive of activity until its closure in 1964. Cattle, chickens, fish, sugar beet and passengers were some of the regular "goods" that came to it. Fields near the line had to be watched for sparks from the steam engines, especially on Sundays when the "Sunday drivers" were blamed for stoking the boilers on the wrong stretch. Many a Sunday dinner was left while fires were beaten out in the corn field.

Other forms of travel, apart from Shanks's pony or bicycles, were horse-drawn vehicles of all kinds, buses, and some motor cars, though not many. Some of the early, pre-war buses were often overloaded and could get overheated and "boil" on the hills. So it was all out and walk up the hill while the driver refilled the radiator, swung the starting handle and the men got

Brandesburton village street, and an early bus waits near the Dacre Arms. (East Riding of Yorkshire Council, Library and Information Services)

ready to push the bus on up to the top. All aboard and merrily on our way.

Cars of the 1930s had running boards, lovely brass lamps and klaxon horns, and some had tops like pram hoods that had to be pulled over in a hurry when it rained. Great fun in a gale. Some two-seaters had a luggage compartment on the back with the wire-spoked spare wheel strapped on the outside. The lid pulled down to reveal a small passenger seat. It was quite unprotected and open to the elements. The proud owners of these cars knew that the engines were so made that they could take them out, strip them down, clean them and put them back in perfect working order. A few spare parts and a weekend's gloriously greasy work and off we went.' *(Ella Musgrove for Fangfoss with Bolton WI)*

▧ OUT ON THE DOCTOR'S ROUNDS ▧

'My father moved into Waldyne House two or three years before the First World War and it is in that house opposite the present

Market Weighton surgery that my memories begin. In my early years I was not aware of my father except as the man who wrote lots of letters to my mother – he was "away at the war" serving on a hospital ship plying between Dover and Calais.

I think it was when or just after he was 40 that my father was released from military service and came home. At first I was most annoyed at this strange man in the house. He would insist much more than mother that I did as I was told. I told him I would send him back to God to make him a woman! After that remark we soon became great pals and remained so until he died in 1958.

Almost every day he used to take me out on his rounds visiting all the villages around Market Weighton, in an open two seater "Star", made in Wolverhampton, with big brass headlamps using acetylene gas provided from a gas machine where water dripped onto carbide. A twin jet burner in front of a large reflector mirror and behind a large lens provided a very powerful beam of light. The side lamps and rear light were paraffin wick lamps. All these took quite a time to light so in the case of a night call-out my father could not be on his way without some delay.

Still it was an improvement on having to wake the groom and get the horse in the trap, which is what he had to do in the late 1890s when my father first came to Market Weighton.

One sad day, about 1916, my father had been to see a patient in Market Weighton before proceeding into the country part of his round. As he cranked up the car (no self starter in those days) there was a slight snap and the engine became lifeless. The timing chain had broken. The factory in Wolverhampton was on war work and it was three years before a new timing chain could be made. This is where a 'T' model Ford comes into my memories.

But it was the dear old Star which I was quite sure was the best car in the East Riding – at any rate for a doctor because it was so reliable. It had a wonderful wind horn with a deep note like a bass trombone. The wind pump worked directly off the flywheel – a Bowden Wire moving the pump wheel up against the

The NER Motor Omnibus Service at Beeford, c1904. (East Riding of Yorkshire Council, Library and Information Services)

flywheel. This, of course, had two snags at least. One, if you were driving slowly in a crowded street the flywheel had not enough revs to sound the horn; unless of course the driver declutched and revved up the engine – then the roar of the engine and the blast of the horn were remarkably effective. Two, going fast on the open road the horn was splendid, but if you required to turn the car round in a limited space the Bowden Wire would get stretched by coiling round the steering column. So one could not avoid a loud long hoot when turning round.

The four cylinder engine was cast in two blocks – my father telling me the factory was not easily able to cast a block big enough for four cylinders in a row.

I have very distinct memories of driving across the green at Newbald and children coming running out calling "motor car – motor car", as many of them had not seen a car.' *(Richard Ashwin, of Londesborough)*

◈ Howdendyke Ferry ◈

'I live in the ancient village of Hook, which may have got its name from the bend in the river. The river is the fast flowing Ouse. After wending its way in a fairly straight line, it takes a sharp left turning towards what many people will be familiar with and that is Boothferry Bridge.

When I was a small child I lived with my parents on the Howden side of the river before the bridge was built. The only way to get across to Goole and the surrounding areas was by crossing the river in a ferry boat, which was rowed across by the ferryman. Anyone who knows the river at this point will realise that this was no mean achievement.

To attract the attention of the ferryman from the Hook side of the river, people had to shout across the wide expanse of water. Competing with the elements in winter was quite a task.

However, the day came when it was decided for us to move to Hook as my father's work was over there. All our furniture was loaded on to the boat, a larger ferry being used for transporting any kind of goods, from sheep and cattle to barrels of beer, motor cars etc.

My mother was very much afraid that everything would end up at the bottom of the river as one or two items were hanging over the side. Anyhow, we must have arrived safe and sound complete with furniture etc. I wonder what people today would have thought of such a journey, and then the walk into the village or further still to anyone wanting to go on to Goole.

A horse bus was available sometime before a motor bus service was started in the late 1920s. Boothferry Bridge was opened in 1929. Many people will be familiar with this bridge as a means of getting to the coast, and it must have seemed a great improvement to the people of the 1920s.' *(Bessie Clarkson – Hook WI)*

◈ Tenting by the Road ◈

'After the enclosure laws were passed and common-held land had been taken from Hook village, rights were given to certain

Crossing by ferry in the 1920s. (Bessie Clarkson – Hook WI)

properties to enable those occupying them to graze cows and horses along the lanes and hedgerows. There were 50 such "lane gates" in Hook. A man was paid for "tenting" (looking after) them. The road between Airmyn and Westfield Bank, for instance, had two gates at either end and the animals would be fastened in the enclosure at night. I remember standing at the gates to open them for people passing from Airmyn to Hook. The system is no longer in use and those whose properties carry a "lane gate" get a small annual rent in lieu.' *(Edgar Hunter, of Hook)*

▣ CATFOSS AERODROME IN THE 1930s ▣

'Every year in the 1930s, on or near 24th May the aerodromes in the UK were opened to the public, and as Catfoss was the nearest to Bridlington where we lived, Dad would take us in his car to see the planes and displays. May 24th was Queen Victoria's birthday and known as Empire Day. All schools had a holiday to celebrate the day and many towns and villages would have fetes and plays performed by schoolchildren to celebrate the occasion.

Catfoss was home to a squadron of biplanes. The pilots flew over the dunes and low cliffs to perfect their ability to shoot at targets towed out at sea by RAF launches from Bridlington, or "shot at" airborne drogues over the sea at Cowden, near Hornsea. It was very spectacular and quite nerve-wracking to see the little planes swooping and diving lower than oneself when I sometimes joined my uncle and aunt at their seaside cottage on the cliffs at Skipsea.

There were aerobatic displays with three biplanes linked together at their wing tips, looping the loop and flying low over the crowds watching. A battery of anti-aircraft guns drilled and fired blank ammunition to demonstrate their accuracy and efficiency and were very noisy in doing so. They frightened my little five year old sister very much, she hid under Dad's mac to shelter from the explosions.

The highlight of my day was the opportunity to climb into the Armstrong Whitley bomber and see the new hydraulic gun turrets working. The aircraft was just in service with the RAF and didn't fly that day but we could look round it. All in all it was quite an experience which we tried to repeat each year, but very soon after that the war broke out and all such freedom was denied us.' *(Shirley Franklin – Driffield WI)*

HOUSE & HOME

The Way We Lived Then

So much has changed since the days water came from the well or pump and there were certainly no 'mod cons'! Goods were delivered to the door by local tradesmen and shopping in the town was a great treat. Our food was usually home-grown and home-cooked – even if it did mean killing the pig ourselves!

▨ More Bother Than They're Worth ▨

'Life was hard for the housewife in 1922. There were some labour saving appliances, but, according to my Granny, "they were more bother than they were worth".

One of the jobs that had to be done every day was bed making – no straightening the sheet and pulling up the duvet, but a full blooded campaign with no short cuts.

Beds had to be "opened" to air as soon as you got out. Then later the bed clothes had to be replaced: straighten bottom sheet, fluff up pillows and lay on top sheet. After the sheets were tucked in, we had to add the blankets – at least two, and the foot-wrap, made from a piece of old blanket and the best bits of old woollen socks and stocks – not smart patchwork but very comfortable for cold feet. The whole array was then covered by a counterpane or a patchwork quilt, depending on the status in the family.

We had two double beds at our house, one for Mum and Dad and one for Granny. We also had two single beds, one for Uncle Stephen and one for me. I helped Granny to make the beds and it took at least half an hour. Granny's bed and Uncle Stephen's bed were pushed up to the wall, so it was very hard to spread and tuck in the covers.

Granny could not leave the child alone downstairs (with an open fire) while the beds were made so I was allowed to "help" – until I grew bored and played with my doll. One day I put her

Little Hilda with the doll Gladys who caused all the trouble! (Hilda
Jackson – Snaith WI)

to bed in Uncle Stephen's bed. Her name was Gladys and she was a beautiful wooden doll with a smart Roman nose. Granny called, "Come on down now." Gladys was fast asleep so I left her in bed.

Uncle Stephen was late home that night and didn't want to disturb the household, so he undressed in the dark and jumped quickly into bed – and sat on Gladys's Roman nose! My Dad said his yell was heard a couple of miles away, but I slept through it all. I couldn't understand why I was then banned from bed-making until my Granny explained it to me.

"Gladys might be in my bed next time," she said with a smile.'
(Hilda Jackson – Snaith WI)

▨ A Clock Ticking ▨

'I only need to hear a clock ticking loudly in a quiet room and I am taken back in time to my childhood home. The home I remember much more vividly than any I have lived in since. Saturday mornings I remember so well. My grandmother, who lived with us, always "did the fireside". This was a big black affair with a side oven. First, my grandmother cleaned the flues, then black leaded the bars and the other black parts, brushing them until they shone. Then the steel edges were cleaned with bath brick and finally the hearth was pointed with whitening.

My Saturday morning job was to clean all the brass door knobs and the brass tap over the sink in the scullery. This sink was shallow and was made of a rough yellow stone material. There was a gas bracket beside the sink and I had to be careful not to whisk my duster near to the fragile mantle. Often I would dust the furniture in the living room – the big horse-hair sofa that was so prickly for bare legs, my grandmother's wooden rocking chair, on which my cousin and I rode to the ends of the earth, and the big, loud ticking clock on the wall.

During the morning the milkman would call with his horse-drawn cart. He would bring his can to the door and ladle out the foaming milk into our jug. Later on the greengrocer would come with his horse drawing a cart full of fruit and vegetables. My grandmother would keep a sharp look out through the lace curtains to see if either of these horses left any droppings. If so I was sent quickly out with a bucket and shovel to collect this invaluable material for the garden. How I hoped that I would not have this job to do!

Sometimes a dirty little old man would come up the back garden path. He carried a tin can fastened to the end of a long stick. This was to clean out the sink in the yard. He would take off the grating and ladle out some horrible black sludge. Was this the only work the poor man ever did? As I watched all this from my secure little world, I little thought that in a few years my father and grandparents would be dead and my mother and I would have to face a harsher world than we had ever known.'
(Marjorie Gedney – Brandesburton WI)

▣ No Mod Cons ▣

'I came to the East Riding in 1953 as a farmer's wife. It was a lovely Georgian house but had no electricity, telephone or drains and poor washing facilities. The implication of this lack of electricity meant that we had to use Tilley or paraffin lamps which had to be filled each day, usually at dusk, the alternative being candles. There could be no electric oven, deep freeze or fridge. No electric fires nor even an electric blanket to air the beds, nor the vacuum to take the mud outside again.

Having no drains necessitated the use of the "three-holer" in the garden shed, with two high seats and one low one.

Finally, the washing was a constant job, everything being washed by hand or posher. The wet washing was then carried down 14 steps to mangle in the cellar, and the water thus extracted had to be carried upstairs and thrown away.

However, we did have hot and cold water through the taps and an Esse stove which kept the kitchen warm and cooked the meals for us when the wind was in the right direction. In those days we had lots of energy and the bigger bonus of all – a happy, healthy family.' *(Anon – Rudston WI)*

'When the old house was wired up for electricity away went the paraffin lamps, candles, and kelly lamps. The set routine of washday didn't alter until some two years later when Rose the wash lady retired.

Rose would arrive at eight o'clock on Monday morning and sit down to a hearty breakfast of eggs, bacon and hot bread cakes, followed by apple pie.

The wash house was separate from the house. The fire was lit under the copper which was filled with rainwater supplied from a large tank. Other equipment consisted of a mangle with wooden rollers, a zinc tub with posher and dolly peg, an oblong wooden tub and a scrubbing board. Reckitts starch and blue bag at the ready, Rose would go into action helped by her daughter, refreshed with a mug of cocoa at eleven o'clock.

The lawn afforded a good drying area, where posts slotted into iron holders and formed a large square. All the washing was finished by midday and time for dinner – meat and vegetables followed by steamed pudding. The washing was then brought in, damped, folded and the sheets put through the mangle ready for ironing. Different sizes and weights of flat irons were heated up on the large range. With three girls who wore starched frocks and underwear, the rack across the ceiling looked quite impressive. Sometimes Rose would be a bit too keen with the starch and the petticoats scratched the neck and the starched knickers made walking a bit painful.

All the ironing finished by five o'clock, Rose sat down to a well earned tea of slices of ham, pickles, home-made bread, and finishing with fruit pie.

She was a super lady but wouldn't touch anything electric with a barge pole. Mother promised herself a washing machine and an electric iron when Rose retired and we had one of the first Hotpoint washers, but we missed Rose and her cheerful face. Mondays were never the same.' *(Janet Isaac - South Cave WI)*

'Washing day was always Monday – and could any day be more dreaded for its upset? The copper lit early, the washing tub and

Flamborough water carriers early in the century. (East Riding of Yorkshire Council, Library and Information Services)

dolly tub all brought in, a small bath for rinsing, and the mangle to test your muscles. Clothes were scrubbed, dollied, boiled, rinsed, blued and starched. A wet day was to be dreaded, as all the clothes hung from lines across the kitchen to dry. All were then damped, neatly folded ready for ironing with flat irons heated on the open fire (and a cloth nearby for making sure they were clean). The clothes, folded again, were then hung to air on lines across the kitchen. Often the meal for the day would be cold meat from Sunday's joint and bubble and squeak.

Bath night was always Friday. A bucket of water was put in the oven to get hot, a tin bath brought in from the shed and put in front of the fire. The fireplace also had at its side a small boiler from which you could ladle out warm water for ordinary washing or washing up. This was always kept filled. Other than that, hot water came from a kettle heated up on the fire.

There were very few water closets. Toilets consisted mostly of a very nicely scrubbed wooden seat with a bucket underneath, and newspaper cut into neat squares for wiping. The emptying of the bucket was often your responsibility. We had no garden but did have an allotment away from the house. My uncle would get up early (hopefully before others), take the bucket to the allotment, dig a big hole and empty the contents, then return home as quickly as possible.' *(M. Winter – Roos WI)*

▦ CLIPPED RUGS ▦

'My mother always had a clipped rug in front of the hearth in the living room, and one in front of the kitchen sink as they wore well on the red brick floors. Making a clipped rug was a job during the long winter evenings. A hessian sack from the farm was unpicked at the seam and washed. It was then stretched taut over a wooden frame by nailing it. The "clips" were strips of material about four inches long and an inch wide cut from old coats, skirts or trousers. This was sometimes my job, and did it make the forefinger sore with pressure from the scissors!

The tool used was often a wooden clothes peg cut down the centre, but a pegging tool could be made from a piece of wood about four inches long and as thick as a finger, with a point at one end. The strip of material or clip was folded in half and pushed tightly into a hole previously made in the sacking. I remember most of our rugs had a four or five inch border in a plain colour, then the centre was filled in with a motley of colours. If a pattern was required this had to be drawn on the hessian first and the clips kept in piles of separate colours. The patterned ones required a bit more concentration. A hessian backing was usually sewn on to make them wear better on the hard floors. As you can imagine, they were no light weight to shake!' *(Audrey Race – Hedon WI)*

▦ THE FARMHOUSE KITCHEN ▦

'At the turn of the century farmhouses with running hot and cold water were as rare as unicorn droppings. The washing up was done in a bowl (kept on the table for the purpose). Hot water was ladled from the side boiler on the kitchen range and the plates and dishes turned out onto an enamelled tray. It was a common practice if there were any sticky or gunged up dishes which

The interior of a cottage at Easington, Hull, c1900. (East Riding of Yorkshire Council, Library and Information Services)

needed soaking, to plunge them in the pump trough and forget about them until needed. It was the lazy way out. One way of passing the buck and leaving someone else to clean the dish.

Enter the kitchen by the back door and you would see the red brick floor shining in the glow from the kitchen fire. A long, deal, well scrubbed table stood under the window and a bench went behind it to facilitate seating arrangements at mealtimes. I know that it was well scrubbed. I did it myself every Saturday and many times in between. Saturday was a day for scrubbing. Everything got scrubbed, whether it moved or not!

When we had any men living in, the men ate at that table and the ladies had a round table to themselves. Two or three wins or chairs, and a number of straight backed oak chairs completed the seating plus an odd stool or two. A painted cupboard housed the everyday crockery, 'llowance mugs and condiments and cutlery. A large and ugly looking bin was there by necessity. It housed the flour, which was always purchased in ten-stone bags. The flour vanished at a fine rate. Batches of bread and pastry were made twice weekly with a supply of cakes and fancies being produced on Fridays ready for the Sunday extra treats.

Food was always very important in our lives and Mum was a marvellous cook, having spent some period of her life as a cook in gentleman's service. I suppose that was about the only employment there was in those days. I heard her talk about being a cook, though I don't really know where she worked and people used to say that she could make things taste like "something else again". When she cooked game, ie pheasant, hare or venison, she knew all the proper accompaniments, like jugged hare with port wine gravy. Pheasant on the menu – my mouth waters now at the thought of it. If a bird got too cheeky round the farmyard, somebody would take a pot shot at it, so we often had one.

All cooking was done in the oven or on the open fire, and of necessity we always had a fine selection of grimy bottomed pans. As I remember, a big steamer pan constantly needed renewing because of a burnt out bottom. A huge frying pan with a handle over the top hung on a bar over the fire. Father was an expert cook. Saturday tea, after a weekly visit to York market was very often cod steaks cooked in this pan. Delicious! We sometimes had smokey flavoured tea, if the fire was not burning too well and the fumes got into the kettle.

Next to the fireplace in the big kitchen was a door which opened into the cupboard under the stairs. A stairway went out of the kitchen to a single bedroom – the lad's room: used mainly when we had a lad living in. This cupboard could be more correctly described as "the Glory Hole". The boys would open the door and whang in working boots and leggings (pre wellington days!), working jackets usually followed suit and mingled with a collection of sweeping brushes and shoe cleaning requisites. All jumbled in glorious disarray.

One memory I have of this "hole" is when at party times ten or a dozen kids would scramble in to watch a "Magic Lantern" show. This was a lantern-like affair lit by candle power and with a supply of coloured slides which were put through an aperture and the picture focused onto the limewashed cupboard wall. A most hilarious time was had by all, but it didn't do much for the girls' party dresses or little boys' tidy suits!

Going into the farmhouse the first thing to catch the eye was a stag's head, its imposing antlers well and truly adorned with a selection of flat caps, trilbys and maybe the odd bowler hat or collar and tie, its enigmatic and baleful eye saying, "Look at me, I'm the Monarch of the Glen and I dislike intensely being used as a common old hat stand." All the boys used to come in and pitch their caps on to a horn as if they were playing hoop-la at a fairground.

There was another stag's head in the front passage but this one was treated with more respect. Nestling below it was an oak gun cupboard. This contained three double-barrelled shotguns, two .303 rifles, one .202 rifle and a four ten airgun. Quite a mini arsenal. A bit much for a farmhouse although most farmers owned a shotgun. The rifles could quite legitimately be called "tools of the trade". They were used when it was necessary to cull any animals from the Deer Park, which was situated in Aldby Park, Buttercrambe.' *(Daisy Naylor – Stamford Bridge WI)*

▣ LIFE AT BARMSTON ▣

'Living on the coast as we did at Barmston, there was often useful fuel washing up on the beach. Often I would spend an hour or more on the beach with my father before breakfast collecting wood or coal. Sometimes there would be heavy pieces of wood like pit props and we would yoke ourselves to them with ropes and drag them along the beach. After tea, these would be sawn into logs, and I would help by stacking them up ready for blazing winter fires.

Once there were boxes of lard washed up and everyone was kept busy melting it down in saucepans on top of cookers. Another time a very large quantity of coal was washed up and the whole village seemed to come to the cliff top. One member of a family would stand guard over their pile while others ferried the treasure trove back to the village in every possible cart and wheelbarrow. Sea coal burnt very well and gave out a good heat, besides being free.

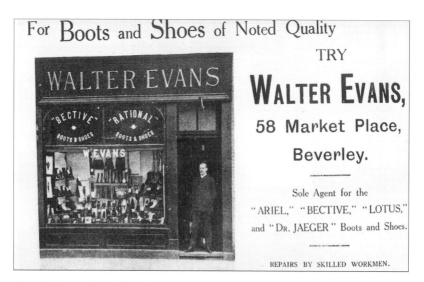

(East Riding of Yorkshire Council, Library and Information Services)

We kept a pig too, and another job was to go with Dad to neighbours and the nearby cafe and caravan site to collect left over bread, vegetable peelings etc for the swill to feed the pig. When the time came for the pig to be killed there was the tub and creel to be fetched from the farm. Again human horses were roped to the load. The butcher came to us and the pig was dispatched outside the back door. Mother and I always went to the farthest side of the bungalow and covered our ears till the deed was done, but afterwards there were buckets of boiling water to be taken outside to fill the tub where the bristles were scraped off the pig. A bowl full of blood for black puddings would have to be stirred. The following day the butcher returned to cut up the pig, and there were pies and sausages to make, and parcels of fry to be delivered to the neighbours.

I learned to skin a rabbit, and pluck a chicken as well as how to make brawn from the pig's head. Nearly everything was home-made or home-grown that appeared on our table. No one had heard of ready meals. Of course, there were things like corn flakes and shredded wheat and Camp coffee (a concentrated liquid in a bottle), but in general the things we ordered from the

(East Riding of Yorkshire Council, Library and Information Services)

grocers were basic foodstuffs which had to have something done to them to produce a meal. The traveller who called once a week used to fascinate me. He rode a bike round the villages, calling regular as clockwork whatever the weather, and rattled off the list of stock to prompt my mother's order – "salt, pepper, vinegar, tea, sugar, flour, suet, lard…" through to "starch, Silvo and furniture polish". He'd write down the order and the delivery van would come another day.

There was also a butcher, a fishman and a bread man who called weekly. We didn't have fridges then, so meals were determined by the arrival of these salesmen. The breadman started bringing ice cream in an insulated container. I can remember arriving home from school one day and being told there was a surprise in the front bedroom. My mother seemed to be bursting with excitement. I couldn't see what all the fuss was about. There was something sloppy and white in a fruit dish. "It's ice cream," said Mother – the first I could remember tasting as I was only a baby when the war began. (The front bedroom was the coolest place – away from the sun – and as the breadman had called not long before I was due home she had hoped it would keep firm long enough.) I was not impressed. It must have been about the same time I first saw a banana as well.

In 1958 "home-made" was still the thing both for food and fashion. I made my own wedding dress and veil and head-dress, plus my going away hat, and we catered for 100 guests at our reception in the village hall. Home-cooked ham, tongue, trifles, cakes and pastries were baked in the little Baby Belling cooker that Mother had been lucky enough to obtain when we had moved to Barmston a few months before the end of the war. She had gone to the Electricity Board to enquire how long a waiting list there was, for things were in very short supply, but to her surprise was told there was one in stock. She immediately paid a deposit and when she returned a few days later with the balance was told that had she not paid the deposit she would not have got the cooker. What would we have done if she hadn't got it I don't know, as there was no other means of cooking. At our previous house we had a side oven so had nothing to take with us.

For washing there had been a copper at the old house. Here there was nothing so Mother spent many cold washdays in the "garage" with her coat on, wielding the dolly stick in the wash tub and wringing out the clothes with the heavy mangle. There was no water supply in the garage so the water supply had to be carried in buckets from the kitchen.

There was no car in the garage either for we never had one, but it served as coal-house and bike shed and vegetable store as well as wash house.

After I married, my washing facilities were only just one step up from what Mother had. Our first home, a ground floor flat, had only gas in the kitchen so I had a gas boiler, but it made so much steam I used to manhandle it out into the yard and feed the connecting tube through the window. The wringer, a lighter model than Mum's, attached to the sink, and of course for both of us, wet washdays meant steaming clothes horses round the fire.' *(Audrey Bemrose – Barmston WI)*

▧ SOMETHING TO REMEMBER ▧

'Invite a group of ladies to spend an afternoon talking and sharing memories and you find that you have really started something. Memories came so thick and fast that some escaped completely.

Joan remembered going with her Grandad to get water from the village pump at Dunnington near York. This was in the late 1930s. Her family lived out of the village and had a pump over the sink (like so many other rural properties) and a well in the garden. Her grandparents lived in the middle of the village and had to use one of the five or so communal pumps scattered around the village. Most farms and villages had pumps and/or wells and piped water was not universal until some time after the war. Water was heavy and precious. (It still is.) On washdays it had to be fetched, poured into a copper, and boiled by the fire underneath. Usually this copper was in a washhouse in the yard, but sometimes it could be in the corner of the kitchen, which became full of steam. The fire took care of most of the household rubbish – there were no wheely bins then.

Fabrics were all natural until after the war, and each type had to have its own special treatment. Rainwater, from storage tanks, was deemed best for washing, and the soapy or rinse waters were not wasted. Floors, tables, steps, yards were all scrubbed and of course step edges and risers had to be donkey-stoned using a sandstone block.

Before piped water and main drains came there was all the fun of earth closets. A single-seater was a luxury, as some of the older ones had two, three or more seat holes in a wooden bench. They were all sited at a respectable distance from the house which meant that if "needs must" on a dark wet night it was heads down and make a rush for it. We heard the mind-boggling tales of someone who sat down on someone who was there already, and of another who was bitten by a resident rat. If you had sole possession there were tantalising snippets of news to read from the squares of newspaper strung up beside you.' *(Ella Musgrove for Fangfoss with Bolton WI)*

▨ Life in Hull ▨

'Shops in Hull during my early life and school days gave personal service. On my seventh birthday I bought a black leather, gold trimmed autograph album from a small shop near Newland Park on Cottingham Road owned by a Mr Benson Brown. He asked me to leave it with him overnight, and when I collected it he had written my name in Old English calligraphy – and painted a delicate water colour of a sailing ship!

I remember a small shop further along which was called Milson's near the Marist College, and which sold cheap sweets. All those childish treats of four gob-stoppers for a penny, sherbet dabs, and long liquorice boot laces.

"In Town", where we travelled by train (a halfpenny fare for school children), the big stores were elegant. Chairs were provided at the mahogany counters, and polite assistants went to much trouble to display goods requested. The cash machines whirled to and fro overhead, with change being whizzed back in

The Bridlington branch of William Cussons Ltd, one of those wonderful high class grocers who seemed to sell everything. (Isobel Shepherdson – Stamford Bridge W1)

little containers opened by the assistant. My mother always requested, "Will you enter this purchase please?" as she preferred to pay monthly.

The Maypole or Liptons were shops selling all kinds of groceries, including dairy products with men and women in overalls slapping butter into half pounds, or whatever weight required, and wrapping it in greaseproof paper. Sugar was weighed into strong blue paper bags. I never saw any goods ready wrapped. Milk was delivered to the house, but in large churns in a horse-drawn cart, and one took jugs out to be filled by a pint measure dipped in the churn.

When shopping with Mother there was time to go into Fields Cafe for a pot of tea, and cream cakes. They did a speciality sponge with peach slices wedged between thick whipped cream. A strong aroma of freshly roasting coffee pervaded. Sometimes as a treat we had afternoon tea in the cafe of the Cecil cinema – where a string orchestra played under palm trees, or potted palms to be exact.

Browns the book shop was a favourite place for browsing, and we chose the "William" books for birthday presents, with annuals at Christmas. Later we chose calf-covered classics with gilt edges, and ribbon bookmarks for 3/6d. Fountain pens, and propelling pencils were also popular presents. My box of Windsor and Newton water colours (in the 1930s) were treasured, and cost 12/6d, very expensive. I replaced it in 1975 and paid £28!' *(Irene Megginson – Bishop Wilton WI)*

'I remember gas lighting in the streets of Hull – watching the lamplighter go down the street on a bicycle balancing a long pole and lighting each lamp as he went along. Children often hung ropes round the lamp-posts from the two arms which stretched out from the top and they made wonderful swings. In those days children in towns played in the streets with marbles, skipping ropes, home-made wheelbarrows and "bogies" made from odd planks of wood and the wheels from old prams.

All the local tradesmen used carts drawn by horses. Boys like my older brother became errand boys during the summer holidays, delivering groceries, riding a bicycle specially adapted to carry huge boxes in front of the handlebars. This was how they earned their pocket money.

A knife grinder came along once or twice a year pushing a sort of handcart which carried the grinding wheel – the children used to crowd round, fascinated. As well as the baker delivering cakes and bread in a basket loaded from his van, there was the milkman, who measured out the milk from a pail into your jug as you stood at the door waiting for him each morning. I remember an old Dutchman came regularly with a basket over his arm, selling dusters, teacloths, etc. Mother was always sorry for him and gave him a cup of tea and a hot pie if she had just been baking, which she did often as she baked all the bread and cakes we ate. The greengrocer, a jolly country man, was my favourite because he often gave me a lift to school after lunch on his horse-drawn cart and sang funny songs to me as we jogged along. My mother had known him since he was a boy and so could trust him to take care of me. He had a little girl of his own and she occasionally came on his rounds with him during the summer holidays.

By this time we had moved to the outskirts of East Hull, to a new house on a housing estate built by a Trust especially for working men and their families, rented of course. The houses were equipped with electricity – no gas. Mother was so proud of her electric kettle, electric clothes boiler, electric oven, a bathroom with constant hot water. We did, however, have a side oven in the fireplace where Mother made the most lovely bread twice a week. Cakes and pies were made in the electric oven, and she was a very good cook.' *(Joan Holt – Cottingham Green WI)*

⊠ KILLING THE PIG ⊠

'This was an annual custom, especially for farmers and cottagers. The farmers would keep pigs for marketing and breeding, and sometimes with a litter of pigs there would be a reckling. This was usually given to a workman to rear at home, and with tender loving care it would make a good bacon pig.

All edible household waste, surplus vegetables and potatoes were always boiled and mixed with corn meal to feed the pig. They usually weighed 20 to 25 stones when killing took place between November to March. Preparations were made in advance. A large block of salt had to be grated finely, saltpetre bought for the curing, a date fixed with the butcher. The copper was filled with water and wooden laths were placed on the pantry or out-house floor. The pig was given only water on the day before it was killed.

On the fixed date the copper fire was lighted to get the boiling water. The butcher would arrive with his tools and large scalding tub. The dead pig was put in the large wooden tub and scalded, the butcher and helpers scraped all the hairs off. The offal was kept, the intestines were put into salted water to clean. If required the blood would be saved for making black pudding. The pig would hang up in an outside place for the night.

The next day the butcher came to cut the pig into joints – hams, shoulders, sides, heads, trotters and chine. All the off cuts were taken to the kitchen, where the women set to work. Leaves of lard were cut up and rendered, the lard being stored in buckets. Pig fry's were given to friends and neighbours, the fry consisting of liver, heart and small pieces of pork.

The best cuts of pork were minced for pork pies, the coarser cuts minced with white bread and seasoning for sausages. The intestines were scraped and cleaned and soaked in clean salted water; these were the sausage skins. Hams and shoulders had saltpetre pushed into the joints and were laid on the wooden laths and covered with salt, with the other pieces. After three weeks the salt was scraped off and the pork washed and dried by hanging it up in the kitchen. When dry it was placed into clean pillow cases and stored in an airy place.

Pork pies were made with hot water pastry, sausages were made by pushing the skins on a funnel fixed on the mincer, all delicious food. The chaps (jaws) were roasted and eaten cold, spare ribs were finger licking good. After being salted the head, trotters, tongue and tail were made into brawn. The chine (backbone) was salted and used later for large roasting joints. The flitches were sometimes rolled and sliced for frying. Ham and shoulder joints were usually soaked and boiled, delicious! The lard was used for baking. A lot of hard work and a good supply of food for a year.

This custom still took place well into the 1950s, but today with refrigerators and freezers so easily available this tradition is no longer needed.

An old country saying was – nothing of the pig is ever wasted, only its squeal. I think you will agree.' *(Marie Grice – Bainton WI)*

REMEDIES AND SUPERSTITIONS

Calling the doctor was an expensive luxury before the National Health Service, and many families relied on tried and trusted remedies for first aid and home cures. And how many superstitions we believed in, that touched every corner of our lives!

▨ CALLING THE DOCTOR ▨

'My parents went to live at Garton in Holderness in 1936, Martinmas time. I was eleven years old, my sister nine years old. The doctor was Dr Whitehead and he lived at Roos, and had a surgery there and at Aldbrough.

There were no telephones in the village except at Grimston Hall. When anyone was ill, we used to go to the cottage at the T-junction, and ask the lady who lived there if she would put a plate in the window for the doctor, so he could see it when he passed by between surgeries.

The doctor would call, ask who needed him, visit them, then

go into his surgery, make up the medicines, and leave them at the cottage on his way back.

This all worked very well, otherwise it was a three mile cycle ride to Aldbrough or a four mile cycle ride to Roos. There were no local bus services then and few private cars.' *(Kathleen Forsey – Elloughton cum Brough WI)*

▣ HOME CURES ▣

'Some home cures were so dire that they were more to be dreaded than the ailments they were supposed to help. Goose grease on the chest or back was supposed to help chesty coughs. Sometimes it was rubbed straight on to the skin or it could be put onto brown paper and that was applied. It crackled when you coughed!

Great trust was placed in Thermogene. I know from experience that if both Thermogene and the new-fangled Vick Vapour Rub were applied at the same time they did not speed the cure, far from it, because the blisters took quite a while to heal.

Drops of camphorated oil were put onto sugar lumps to help sore throats, or chunks of swede dipped in demerara sugar. Buttered boiled onions, or lemon, honey and vinegar in hot water, were pleasant. A sweaty sock wrapped around the throat was not.

Friday night was castor oil or syrup of figs night, with much nipping of noses and in goes the spoon.

And lovely Spring Medicine? Home made lemonade – the fizz being supplied by a large dose of Epsom Salts!' *(Ella Musgrove, for Fangfoss with Bolton WI)*

'My father swore by cornflour mixed with cold water to cure diarrhoea – it was supposed to thicken the contents of the stomach and "bind it together"!

At the start of a cold it was a mug of hot milk and treacle, sometimes hotted up with a dash of pepper, drunk as hot as possible before going to bed.

Brimstone (flowers of sulphur) and treacle were mixed in a cup and a spoonful taken each morning to clear spots in spring.

Jane Turnbull at the front door of her cottage in East Street, Kilham in about 1900. (Margaret Parker – Kilham WI)

Fully dressed for a picnic on the beach at Bridlington in the 1920s.
(Shirley Franklin – Driffield WI)

Grandad, who lived well into his eighties, had a raw egg beaten up in milk every morning – no signs of salmonella then!

Grandma relied on Beecham Pills and Beecham Powders as cure-alls for everything and always had a supply in her handbag when she visited. Zinc ointment for soothing and boracic ointment for "drawing" were standards in the first aid box.'
(Audrey Bemrose – Barmston WI)

❖ ALL HER OWN REMEDIES ❖

'I have a small notebook that belonged to my grandmother. Her sister, Ellen Davy, was a nurse and midwife who worked in the Beverley area attending births and living in during confinements up until the early 1950s. Aunt Nellie made all her own mixtures, salves and ointments using ingredients which were delivered to her cottage in Thearne each week by Goldspink's the chemist in Butcher Row, Beverley. Some of the ingredients are very much in use today, but I have no idea what opperdildock, Wakefield Drops and turkey rhubarb are. As a child I was always given her raspberry vinegar to drink (an eggcupful at a time) whenever I had a sore throat, and we always had a tin of her All Heal Ointment on the go. Looking back, I am sure more germs must have been added to the tin by unwashed fingers than were kept out of the wound.

Here are some of her recipes:

Bronchitis – 1 tablespoonful of ipecacuanha wine, 2 tablespoonfuls of honey, 2 tablespoonfuls of lemon juice. First melt the honey and then add the other ingredients.

Salve for a bad breast – 1 tablespoonful of cream, white of one egg, 1 teaspoonful of glycerine. Beat up to a white paste.

For pains in body – 1oz Wakefield Drops. Half teaspoonful in warm water and sugar.

Indigestion – 1d turkey rhubarb, 1d ground cinnamon, 1 piece of saltpetre the size of a bean. Put in a gill of water and simmer on the fire and bottle.

White Oils – 1 gill of best spirits of turpentine, 1 gill of white vinegar, 2d of "Saudmman" (sic), 2d of opperdildock, white of 2 eggs and the yolk of one. Beat up the eggs, add the other ingredients. Put into a bottle and shake well.' *(J. Wilson – Kilham WI)*

▣ So Many Superstitions ▣

'These are just some of the superstitions I remember:

Birth –
When my son was born in 1943 an old lady gave him an egg, pinch of salt, a match and some money.

It was considered unlucky to visit anyone after childbirth until one had been churched and the baby christened.

The baby should go up before being taken downstairs so it would rise in the world.

Babies' finger nails should not be cut – bitten if they grew too long.

If the baby was born in hospital the mother's bed should be stripped before she left, or she would be back in it in a year (did the nurses encourage this to help them with their work?).

Childhood –
When a child lost a milk tooth, the tooth was sprinkled with salt, wrapped in paper and burnt.

A child with whooping cough was taken on the Hull Ferryboat to New Holland, or taken to the local gas works.

Marriage –
Unlucky to be married in May – I was married on April 30!

Best man should be a bachelor in case the bridegroom didn't turn up and then he could marry the bride.

The bride should wear "something old, something new, something borrowed, something blue", and should not wear green.

Three times a bridesmaid, never a bride.

Death –
Curtains were drawn until after the funeral and were also drawn by all the neighbours in the street at the time of the funeral. All the family attended church or chapel the Sunday after the funeral. Black was worn – clothes could be dyed for funerals. Dyers undertook dying orders for funerals. Black armbands were worn for a time, or a black diamond stitched on coats. I had a black diamond stitched on my coat when grandma died in 1935.

Death omens – pigeon sitting on a roof, dogs howling.

When a plate of pig fry (pig cheer, it was called) was given to a neighbour after pig-killing, it was unlucky if the plate was washed afterwards – the hams and bacon wouldn't keep well.

It was unlucky for a pregnant woman to help with the work of the pig-curing etc for the same reason.

After a cow had calved a jug of the first milk (bislings or beastings) was given to neighbours with instructions that the jug had not to be rinsed or washed out.

My father didn't like twin calves, the heifers were supposed to be infertile. He also disliked all white calves. My mother wouldn't have hawthorn flowers (May) or Quaking Grass brought into the house and didn't like peacock feathers. If the hens laid a small egg at the beginning or end of a laying season it couldn't be brought inside and was usually thrown away.

A rabbit's foot carried in the pocket brought good luck.

A coin turned (and spat upon) and a wish made when the cuckoo was first heard.

A wish made when the new moon was first seen shouldn't be told to anyone. It was unlucky to see a new moon through glass (what if you wore glasses!).

Mother wouldn't wear anything green – she said when she had done she had to have it dyed black for a funeral.

A knife dropped meant a "big man coming".

A piece of tea leaf floating at the top of a cup was a stranger coming and a black piece of soot on the fire bar could mean a stranger or a coffin.' *(Eileen Green – Cottingham WI)*

CHILDHOOD & SCHOOLDAYS

Memories of Childhood

Those who grew up in the first half of the 20th century have memories of simple games and pleasures, of the excitement of a trip to the fair or the seaside, and of the freedom of childhood which, sadly, many of today's children never experience.

▨ Ten in the Family ▨

'I was born in November 1897 at Bowthorpe Hall Farm, Skirlaugh. My father was farm foreman for Thomas Holtby. There were ten of us in the family. We had to walk a mile and a half to school every day, and there were no school dinners. No cars or buses on the roads either, only horse-drawn carts and traps, carriers' wagons and steam rollers. Our only entertainment was to listen to records on the old type of gramophone you had to wind up. How we enjoyed it. Then came the wireless after the First World War and how wonderful that was, to put on the headphones and listen to foreign stations and the London dance bands. My father would not listen to or touch the wireless. He said, "I don't hold with these new-fangled things."' *(Mrs S.J. Bryant – Welton cum Melton WI)*

▨ Magic Moments ▨

'My earliest recollection is of being on the sands at Pitt's Wall with our nurse. We spent every day, weather permitting of course, on the sands at Bridlington with our buckets and spades and with our dresses tucked into our knickers; no T-shirts and shorts in those days! One afternoon we were playing and a big dark shadow crossed the water and beach. It was a very large airship, either the R100 or R101 which had their base at Howden in a huge hangar, still there today. The year was 1929-30 and she was called the "Mauritania of the Air".

80

In the early 1900s babies were kept in long gowns for the first six months or so, and then went into 'frocks' – this is young Albert at the age of three. Eventually the frock would be passed down to his sisters, after the hem had been let down as far as it would go! (Audrey Race – Hedon WI)

If we did not spend the afternoon on the beach, we would picnic and play games on Bessingby Fields and in the summer the Royal Artillery had a training camp there. When the soldiers exercised the horses which hauled the limbers and large guns, Nurse and her helpers would hurriedly collect toys, children and toddlers into the large prams to get out of the way of the thundering hoofs and gun carriages.

When we were on the sands and my brother Bob was missing, Nurse always knew where he could be found – stood transfixed watching a disabled Great War Veteran playing a harp for money to supplement his pension; this was on the south side of Bridlington where we lived.

In 1931 we moved to Sands Lane on the Northside very close to the sea and beach, where again we spent many happy hours. Sometimes we sat watching the Pierrots in their black and white costumes – a pleasant hour or so's entertainment with a piano, Max and Maxine who sang love duets and danced, a funny man, a juggler, a tumbler and songs from the latest shows and radio. "Tiptoe thro' the tulips" and "Painting the sky with sunshine" were two favourites. We also admired the artist who painstakingly created wonderful pictures with coloured sand and chalk on the flat beach, only to have it washed away by the next high tide.

One evening in July 1935 my father, who had returned home from his office in Hull, collected all five of us, much to the disapproval of Nurse who ruled the bedtime of the children with a rod of iron. He wrapped us up in blankets and warm dressing gowns and took us to the balcony of our home which overlooked the Bay to see the passing by of the SS *Mauritania* – all her lights blazing, a wonderful sight on her way to Rosyth to the breaker's yard. Dad had seen her launched at Newcastle in 1907 when thousands turned out to watch such an event, she was a beautiful ship and it was a magical moment for all us children.

When I was eleven years old, my ten year old sister Hilary and I were taught to swim by Mr Gautier, a remarkable man who dived into the sea off the harbour wall tied in chains – à la Houdini! We learnt to swim in his swimming pool somewhere near the harbour side. We were over-awed by his daring deeds and impressed as he only had one arm!' *(Shirley Franklin – Driffield WI)*

▨ Life on an Isolated Farm ▨

'I was born in 1929 in an isolated farm cottage at a place called Swine Carrs. I was the eldest of three children, my father was a farm foreman and we had three hired farm workers "living-in". The house was really two cottages made into one, the farmworkers living in one half being looked after by my mother and eating with us in our half. The workers were hired by my Dad at the Hull Market on Martinmas Day and they came for a year. Their duties included looking after the cart horses which were used for all the farm work. These were very gentle creatures and I can remember my three year old sister causing a scare once by walking under one of these very large horses but it stood perfectly still until she was safe.

My childhood was happy. My brother and I played in the fields, the stackyard and the granary, sometimes just the two of us and sometimes with the boys from the next farm and so I became quite a tomboy. If we got into any mischief it was dealt with quickly and decisively by my father, no tea and bed! We helped to take lunches to all the workers during the harvest and on threshing days. We had extra help for the harvest from the Irish workers who came back every year and slept on the granary floor. Threshing days were very exciting, the noise of the steam engine waking us very early in the morning. It was a very busy time, noisy, dusty and with lots of mice to chase as they escaped from the corn stacks. Another of my tasks was to fetch the milk every day from the farm which was across two fields and I had to be very careful not to spill any from the cans on the way back.

I started school when I was four, riding my bike the one and a half miles to the village. On Wednesdays my mother used to meet us from school and we were given a halfpenny to spend and on Saturdays we had a penny pocket money which we

Off on a school trip from Atwick to Hornsea in 1906. (Marie Grice – Bainton WI)

usually spent on sherbet, aniseed balls or licorice. Sometimes on a Saturday my mother and I would walk to Swine station, with my sister in the pram, and we would catch the train to Hull to go shopping down Whitefriargate and then have chips at Carvers in the Market Place. This was a canvas stall where you sat on wooden benches. There was clean sawdust on the floor and the chips tasted wonderful. We would then catch the train back to Swine and walk home in time for tea. My grandparents lived at Skirlaugh and on fine Sundays we would all cycle to see them. My Grandad was a groom at Dowthorpe Hall. He was a very strict man and I was quite scared of him but he taught me to clean shoes properly. My Grandma was kind and gentle and in awe of Grandad whose word was law. She was usually dressed in black and I have a valued framed photo of her looking very elegant.

In 1938 we had moved into the big farmhouse which had been standing empty as no new tenant had been found – in the days before the war no one wanted to rent Crown farms. I loved this house with its big spacious rooms, a beautiful garden full of flowers and shrubs and in the spring an orchard that was a glorious mass of daffodils. It was in this house that I remember hearing Neville Chamberlain announce that we were at war with Germany. We didn't really understand what it all meant but I can remember that my mother cried. My dad built an air-raid shelter, in the house, of railway sleepers which would have probably killed us all if the roof had fallen in. He also made a room that could have been sealed off if there was a gas attack. At Swine we were in direct line with Stoneferry and after the night Reckitts was bombed there were burnt papers blowing all over the fields. One night we had all our front windows blown in and there were several bombs dropped in the fields, including one which did not explode. We wanted to go and look at it but Dad wouldn't let us!

The headmistress at Swine school was a lovely lady called Mrs Young (a real Jean Brodie). She gave me extra lessons after school and with her encouragement I won a scholarship in 1940 to go to a grammar school. My parents were very proud and happy for me and I was allowed to choose my favourite tea (tinned salmon and tinned pears). So I started going to Malet Lambert High School, travelling by train to Sutton and walking the rest of the way. This was a whole new world to me but I soon settled down, made friends and loved it there.' *(Joan Reed – Leven WI)*

▨ WHAT A GRANNY SHOULD LOOK LIKE ▨

'I was five years old when my family came back to Britain and both sets of grandparents had died so I never knew them. However, I do remember a neighbour of ours, a dear old lady who lived alone and she was just what I thought a "Granny" should look like.

She was small and very round and always wore a large clean white starched apron tied at the back with a big bow. She reminded me of a roly-poly pudding in a big white cloth. Her face was round and apple cheeked. She had two chins that wobbled when she laughed, and her hair was snow white and done up in a neat little bun at the back of her head.

Her cottage was small and had oak beams, and hanging from the beams were herbs of various kinds and dried flowers. My favourite room was the kitchen. It had a big black cooking range with a bright fire burning. She did all her baking in the side oven, lovely-smelling fresh baked bread and cakes. She was always bustling about singing to herself.

In her younger days she had been a Nanny so she loved children and they loved her. Other children popped in to see her besides me and we were always rewarded with some kind of tit-bit.

She brewed many different kinds of herbs to cure different ailments and I remember neighbours often went to see her for "one of Granny's cures". I don't ever remember Granny being ill and she never seemed to get any older.

After leaving school we moved to another area and I had to say a tearful goodbye to her, promising to keep in touch. We sent birthday cards and Christmas cards for quite a few years, then suddenly they stopped coming. The Post Office returned our cards and told us that Granny had died peacefully at the ripe old age of 90.

I was tempted at one time to go back to the village where I spent part of my childhood days. I knew Granny would not be there but I thought her cottage might be. In the end I decided not to return. I have my memories of "Granny" and her cottage locked away in my memory for ever.' *(A. Bean – South Cave WI)*

▨ SATURDAYS ▨

'Saturdays we helped at home – cleaning the brass taps above the kitchen sink, washing and cleaning the lavatory and cleaning with donkey stone all the steps: back door, shed, lavatory, and front door. Our lavatory was quite modern. Going to my friend's older house, their wooden toilet seat had one small hole and two large holes across the width. It was cleaned out by a night soil man.

Walkington schoolchildren c1910, near the Dog and Duck. (East Riding of Yorkshire Council, Library and Information Service)

Saturday afternoon we went to spend our twopence pocket money on cinder toffee, sherbet dabs, aniseed balls, and scented sweets that said "I Love You", "You Are Pretty" and other sayings. The station platforms had machines where you put a penny or twopence in and got a bar of Nestle's chocolate.' *(Ann Alden – Pocklington WI)*

▨ Out to Play ▨

'Summer holidays were best. After I had washed the breakfast pots I could go out to play. We didn't live far from the Humber Bank so my friends and I would go down there. We took my dog with us and we would play down there nearly all day. We had a swing to play on. We would then paddle about in the mud in our bare feet and have to clean them under a pump. We also had to wash the dog. On our way home we gathered wild flowers from the wood. Mum never used to worry about us. She knew we were safe.' *(Mrs N.M. Nurse – Welton cum Melton WI)*

'How we loved parties in each other's houses at Christmas, or on birthdays. Mothers usually had a friend or relative to assist with organising the games, often with the music of piano, or wind-up gramophone. All the usuals – Grandmother's Footsteps, Here We Come Gathering Nuts in May, Wallflowers, Poor Mary Sat a-Weeping, I Took a Letter to My Mother, Stations and Forfeits. The latter involved spinning a plate which if not caught when your name was called meant giving some little "forfeit" in the way of recitation, song or dance! One well remembered was "Sing in one corner, dance in another, laugh in another, and cry in the last".

Children, mostly girls, were well behaved, and joined in happily. Musical bumps was a favourite, also "hats" and "chairs". "Statues" called for immobility after jigging or dancing till the music stopped. If you moved you were out.

Charades was a team game with much whispering, planning, and dressing up in the hall. The team had to think up a three-syllable word to be acted in four scenes, one for each syllable and then the final word, to be guessed by the other team.

Tea time was a happy meal, all keen to tackle sandwiches of egg or potted meat, iced buns, fancy biscuits like "playtime" or "midget gems", birthday cake, and jellies sometimes with tinned fruit.

My family special consisted of peach halves filled with whipped cream with a glace cherry on top and "handles" of angelica. They looked very pretty set out on large plates. We drank lemonade from bottles (in early childhood) with glass marbles in the neck. I still have the wooden gadget used to press the marble into the grooves to let the liquid be poured out.

Children were called for by relations, or maids promptly at seven o'clock. I never remember any party flagging. We were so enthusiastic, and there was often a quiet period when some bright show offs like me loved to entertain with recitations. We only took presents if it was for a birthday. We also constantly played card games in each other's homes, or chess, draughts or standing on heads, or hands against doors on landings, or whichever room had enough clear space. Shoes removed first, of course!

Out of doors there were ball games. Did anyone else play Egg if You Move? Hopscotch, skipping for hours. I had a hoop, but never a top. We climbed every possible tree in our gardens, and rode cycles around quiet roads, and walked to the Beverley Road baths to swim, crossing Pearsons' Park on the way where we sometimes stopped to look at the birds in the noisy parrot house. I remember the metal drinking cups chained to the water fountain, but we ignored those in a snobbish way, as "only for poor people".

No mothers of any of my friends went out to work so they were usually around the house, or garden, though some led social lives with a maid or two left in the home. My mother drove the family car, and took me with a friend on drives to the sea, moors, or wolds for picnics beautifully packed by "Mother's help" and a little stove kettle was used to make tea. We sat on rugs, often in chalk pits, and never thought of tables and chairs. China cups were well wrapped in damask serviettes. Crustless, thin sandwiches were packed in an aluminium hinged, lidded container, lined with greaseproof paper.

We children (and we were children till aged 14) loved to pick

Welton boys kitted out for an outing in 1919. (Hazel Widd – Welton WI)

wild flowers which grew in profusion in our favourite picnic places, bluebells, primroses, and great bunches of cowslips. We never found any irate farmers, or landowners, but there were many gated roads, and open pasture land.

As we grew older, we could go to the "pictures" on Saturdays, or in the holidays. Sevenpence for a seat, twopence for a Crunchie, or Fry's cream bar, and a halfpenny on the tram. We were avid readers, going through A.A. Milne as new editions came out, then Richmal Compton's "William" books, and all the annuals for both girls and boys. *Rainbow* comics were followed by *School Friend*, and eventually we were hooked on *The Magnet* and *Gem*, becoming entranced by boys' boarding school adventures.

Holidays were scarce in my family as my father was a shopkeeper, and seldom left work in charge of others. An aunt and uncle with a daughter my age sometimes asked me to join them in "apartment" holidays at Scarborough, and I loved that. Imagine the landladies cooking the visitors' own food, and producing meals for two, or three families at midday, with cold high tea at five o'clock.

With pierrots, Punch and Judy, ice cream stalls, and donkey rides we enjoyed the sun (there were hot summers in the 1930s) and the sea. On Sundays we wore best dresses and joined Aunt and Uncle in sedate walks on the South Cliff promenade, gathering speed as we shot on ahead down the winding paths to the Italian Gardens – before reaching the beach, and having the luxury of the cliff tram to take us up to the top road again.

Happy memories!' *(Irene Megginson – Bishop Wilton WI)*

▨ ROMANTIC MEMORIES ▨

'Most of my romantic memories were inspired by the cinema. We often went to the Lounge at Bridlington, always a matinee. The most memorable film was *Romeo and Juliet*, with Norma Shearer and (I think) Robert Taylor, so sad but a fantastic story for a ten year old girl. It's the oddest things that stick in the memory! When we came out of the Lounge our nurse, who was a Norland trained girl and was wearing her pale-grey uniform, had two wet patches on her coat where the tears had run down her face during the very sad ending to the story!

We didn't have comics bought us but I did look at and read Nanny's *Picture-goer* magazine. I was allowed to have the full sized photos of Gary Cooper, Nelson Eddy, Robert Taylor, Spencer Tracey and many others but they had to be pinned up on the wardrobe doors, inside, of course. My "pin-ups" of those far off days!

The war years had a different sort of pin-up. Film magazines were hard to come by so I collected postcards of aeroplanes, ships, tanks and cuttings of national and war-time exploits from the newspapers of the day.

Going to the cinema in Hull was a very elegant affair. Dad's secretary always took Hilary and me to the Cecil or one of the other large cinemas but the overall memory is having afternoon tea brought to us by a waitress. Scones, buttered teacakes and small 'fancies' and of course, tea in a small pot with milk and sugar, cups and saucers in pretty china.' *(Shirley Franklin – Driffield WI)*

▣ A PENNY A WEEK ▣

'I was born in Market Weighton in 1913. I got a penny a week pocket money as a child, and sometimes a penny ha'penny to go to the pictures on Saturday afternoon to see Charlie Chaplin, Jackie Coogan, Snub Pollard etc in a barn-like hall.

Our first radio was "a moving coil" with headphones to listen through. Later we were lucky to have a cabinet receiver with a loudspeaker and all the family and neighbours came one evening to hear *Journey's End*. They all thought it was wonderful.

Most nights after tea in winter we would gather round the fire and Dad would read funny broad Yorkshire stories to us from Clock Almanac, or we would play card games.' *(Clara Rawson – Thorngumbald WI)*

'In the 1930s, on the last Friday at school before breaking up for the summer holidays we all sat in anticipation. We knew the village publican would be coming to distribute the tickets for the trip.

It was almost home time when he came. Every child was given a return rail ticket and one shilling to spend. We took great care of these and quickly took them home. The trip was to Bridlington and it was a once-a-year day as we were never taken out of the village on outings.

The day before the trip preparations began. Sandals were cleaned, cotton dresses and towels put ready for the morning. Mother boiled some eggs until they were hard and we were given the job of peeling and mashing them with butter and seasoning for the sandwiches. We had to get up early to help with chores and errands. Mother would already be making the sandwiches with home-made bread, egg and lettuce from the garden, all packed in a tea towel and then into a basket, with currant pasty. Nothing sticky was taken. We put on our cotton dresses and Mother hers. She also wore a lovely fine straw, powder blue picture hat trimmed with pink and white ribbon, she looked lovely.

Excitement was running high. The train arrived at the station at nine o'clock and we had quite a long way to walk so we started off in good time. The station platform was crowded with children and parents. At last the steam train came chuffing to a halt. Some of the carriages were already full so we had to be quick to find a vacant seat. We watched the guard wave his flag, heard the slow chuff-chuff of the engine, and the driver letting off steam, and then the speed started to build up faster and faster non-stop to Bridlington.

Carrying our sand bucket and the spade we had to share, we made haste to the beach, finding a convenient place usually near the wall to settle down on the towels. We had no swimming costumes so we tucked our dresses into our knickers with a strict warning not to get wet. We loved jumping the waves and daring who could go the deepest with shrieks of laughter and splashing,

In the 1930s prams were made to last! (Marie Grice – Bainton WI)

and yes, we did get wet.

When lunch time came we cleaned the sand from our hands and ate the sandwiches. Mother went to buy a jug of tea with cups from a stall on the beach, returning them when empty for the deposit. The tide would be creeping in so we hurriedly made ourselves respectable and made a hasty retreat. A stiff breeze whipped up while we were walking on the pier watching the boats. Mother gave a cry, "Oh, my hat!" The wind had blown it off and we saw it disappearing over the sea wall. We ran to the edge and peered over just in time to see the lovely hat filling with water and slowly sinking.

We were taken into Woolworths for a quick look round and to spend our shilling. Slowly we walked back to the station. The train left at 5 pm and everyone was tired and much quieter going home. We arrived home about 6 pm after having a very happy day despite the hat. The next year the same thing happened again, and this time the hat was a white linen pull-on type. Mother never wore a hat to the seaside again.' *(Marie Grice – Bainton WI)*

FAIRY CYCLE

No. 1 Ball-bearing Rubber Pedals. Adjustable plated handle bars with cycle grips, ⅞-in. wired-on tyre, 12 in. wheels, cone bearings, adjustable cycle saddle, brake, free-wheel, and mudguards.
PRICE **59/6**

No. 2 With ⅞-in. ribbed tangent spoke, ball-bearing wheels.
PRICE **87/6**

▩ ALWAYS HAM ▩

'As a child, if ever there was a school outing or a picnic we had to have ham sandwiches. We never got ham any other time, it was too expensive, but we had no choice on trips. It was ham. It didn't matter that I wasn't keen on it and would much have preferred egg, or even jam, but no, it had to be ham. Mam would say, "I don't want people thinking we can't afford it." No amount of begging or cajoling would make her change her mind. What Mam didn't know, however, was the number of children who were prepared to swap sandwiches. I'd take anything I could get my hands on, as long as it wasn't ham.' *(Heather Speck – Kilham WI)*

▩ THOSE RECKITTS GIRLS ▩

'I was born in Hull in 1941 and the bill for having a midwife in attendance was 32 shillings. My parents were working class and this princely sum was equivalent to two weeks' rent and groceries for the family. A fortnight later the terrace in which we lived was flattened by one of Hitler's bombs and so we moved to Hessle. Hessle then was a village surrounded by fields, and farming was still part of the economy. We lived down Eastgate, at one end of which Mr Oust kept pigs and at the other end the farm ran a dairy herd.

The Church of England school was at the end of the Hurn and whilst the infant classes were mixed, on reaching seven years old we were segregated into (big) girls and (big) boys school, separate buildings with school yards split by a six foot fence. Mr Andrews was the headmaster in my time, the girls' classes having lady teachers and the boys being taught by male teachers.

Games we played in the yard included marbles, whip and tops, ball and skipping. One skipping rhyme we chanted went, "Reckitts girls, Reckitts girls, eyes like diamonds, teeth like pearls, rosy cheeks and flaxen curls, none can beat those Reckitts girls". On leaving school I went to work at Reckitts so becoming one of their "girls". The firm had a long established policy of caring for the health of its employees with a doctor, dentist and nurses on the payroll. You also had to pass a medical before being accepted for employment there.

On Sundays we attended church service before lunch and Sunday school in the afternoons. Our venue was the Congregational church which boasted a "tin tab" (tabernacle) in its grounds, the latter being used for guides, scouts concerts etc. After Sunday school my brother and I would go for a walk to Hessle foreshore or maybe train-spot from the embankment near Station Road. He kept a note book in which were recorded the locomotives we had seen.

Everything being rationed and in short supply, most of our possessions were secondhand or as it is nicely put nowadays, pre-owned. Our home was sparsely furnished and I slept in a bed with my sister. Our shoes were the one item which were not pre-owned, and were bought on a club cheque which my mother paid back at a few shillings a week. Clothing was handed down and worn until nearly threadbare. My auntie's old dresses were converted to frocks with matching knickers for me, and how I hated those flowered knickers, when we had to strip off to vest and pants in the school yard for PE!' *(Doreen Cocker – Rudston WI)*

▣ A Pig's Bladder ▣

'At Newbald children's games tended to be seasonal. Many pavements were marked out for hopscotch in the summer, and they played conkers in the autumn and bows and arrows in winter.

It was a rarity to see children playing with a proper ball in the early 1920s – a pig's bladder blown up very tight with a bicycle pump was common, especially in Newbald, and very strong balls they made!' *(Richard Ashwin, of Londesborough)*

▣ Going to the Fair ▣

'I can remember going with some friends to stay with an aunt who lived in the country, a distance of about seven miles. There were no buses and we didn't own a car so we went by carrier's cart. We loved these trips to see her, but we were also quite useful. Remember there was no electricity or water in the house so we used to fetch the water in buckets. We were given two buckets and four pieces of wood fixed together to form a square. We went to the village pump, filled the buckets and put them on the ground. Then we placed the square over the buckets with the handles outside – stood in the middle of the square and carried them that way, so that if any was spilt we never got wet. This had to be done more than once a day, as the boiler by the side of the fire had to be kept topped up. We also went to a nearby farm with quite a large can for one pennyworth of skimmed milk, which was made into mouth-watering custards and rice puddings.

I think one of the highlights of our visit was when we went "sticking". My aunt had an old pram and we would all set off for a country walk picking up sticks, which when kept until dry were used for firelighting.

In between we played the usual games, skipping, hopscotch, tig, spinning tops and hide and seek.

We also collected wild flowers, which we identified, pressed between the pages of books and finally stuck into a large exercise book, naming them together with date and place found. How I wish I had some of those books now – what a treasure!

Another great occasion was when the fair came. There were one or two rides and side shows such as roll the penny and hoop-la, and there was a certain sweet sold called "cure all". It was delicious but I never hear of it now. The farmers brought pigs, sheep and cattle to be judged and all in all it was a very friendly social occasion.

As we got a bit older we were allowed to go to the village dance, but as there was no village hall the largest room in the school was cleared of desks and there always seemed to be someone willing to play the piano. Of course there was the usual big supper provided by parents and we were always made very welcome. On other evenings we played draughts, ludo, simple card games and dominoes.

Looking back I realise what a simple but oh, so happy a childhood we had.' *(O. Gabbetis – Hutton Cranswick WI)*

▨ GAMES IN THEIR SEASON ▨

'The games we played had their seasons and changed overnight as if by magic – from whips and tops to hoops (or bowlers) and sticks, for instance. Metal hoops and sticks made a much more satisfactory noise.

There was hopscotch, kick the can, marbles, flicking cigarette cards, swapping cards and comics. And of course there were all the complicated "counted out" rhymes and the rhymes that went with the skipping games. To think we could run in, skip, and chant, all at the same time! Then there were the endless ball games – pig in the middle and complex rituals involving throwing balls or bouncing them against a wall. And Queenie. Remember Queenie? Queenie stood in front of her friends with her back to them. The ball she held was thrown backwards over her head and was quickly concealed, the whole group hiding their hands behind their backs and trying to look angelic.

Queenie had to guess who was hiding the ball. If she was right they changed places, but if she was wrong the ritual was repeated.

Football and cricket and rounders were more team games enjoyed, but with unfortunate results at times. One indelible memory is of a fearsome swipe that sailed through the dairy window into a five gallon vat of cream that was waiting to be churned. Butter and tempers were short that week.' *(Ella Musgrove for Fangfoss with Bolton WI)*

▣ MAKING DO IN THE WAR ▣

'I started school in 1944, and arrangements were made for the headmistress to pick me up on her way from Bridlington to Lissett. There were only a few older children in Fraisthorpe, who went on their bikes to Carnaby school. My mother said there was no way a five year old was going to ride or walk along roads busy with army vehicles etc, especially as it was two or three miles to school in either direction.

So it was that the rector spoke to the headmistress and I travelled in state in her car to and from school for several months until the day we moved house to live at Barmston. In the morning it was the car journey as usual. After school I had to walk the two miles home with the Barmston children. It was January, with a strong wind blowing from the sea. I thought we should never reach home that night. It was several years before school buses began running. We trudged backwards and forwards through the seasons, playing marbles in the gutter, kicking balls or picking celandines and daisies according to season. On wet days the fire guard in the "big room" would be festooned with steaming coats drying round the open fire, and wet shoes would be lined up on the floor, for not everyone had wellies to wear. Once a strange smell drifted round the room – someone's crepe soled shoes had been drying a bit too near the fire, and had begun to melt.

In winter cocoa was made in a tall jug for our playtime break, and in summer we had bottles of milk delivered by a milk lorry which had travelled many miles before it reached us and on hot days it seemed almost on the turn by the time we got it. Yet in the village milk was still delivered by the can, ladled out with half pint or one pint measures into your own jug, or on Sundays I would go straight to the farm with an enamel can made for the purpose (its lid could be inverted to use as a cup) to get our milk.

At school one day a huge wicker basket arrived full of sweets which we shared out amongst us. I think the gift came from American or Canadian airmen. Of course we had had very few sweets during the war because of rationing. Even in August 1950 I was in a fancy dress parade as a washerwoman with a placard saying "waiting for de-rationing of soap".

Rationing and shortages meant lots of "being careful" and "make do and mend". My first set of letters of the alphabet were bent from thick wire by Dad using a pair of pliers, and he used oddments of wood nailed together to make a bed for my teddy bear. When my pot doll fell off the settee and broke her leg, Dad found a suitably curved twig and made her a new one, carving individual toes to match the other foot. Dad was good with bikes too, fitting spare wheels from one into the frame of another, with other bits and pieces saved from somewhere else. A touch of black paint and a bike looked nearly new.

Bikes were an important mode of transport, for hardly anyone owned cars in the late 1940s. We would ride many miles on Sundays to visit relatives in other villages in the area, and would always take some contribution for tea – a home-made cake, or a jar of jam. Then on leaving we would be given flowers from their garden, or gooseberries or blackcurrants to take home with us.'
(*Audrey Bemrose – Barmston WI*)

▨ DORIS ▨

'Doris was our maid. I don't know when she came to Mill House but I became aware of her when I was about five years old. Her home was in the village but she lived in with us. She was about five feet five inches tall, thin, wiry and quick in her movements. Her expression was happy and her bright eyes missed nothing.

Her black straight hair completed the picture of a "Lyon's Nippy" to a tee as she wore a uniform with a white cap. Her skills as a cook she had learnt from her mother, making all the bread and cakes that we needed, but her speciality was inventing puddings which she named after her nieces and nephews. We never met them but Nesta and Brian often took pride of place on our dining table.

On winter evenings, work done, our favourite place was the kitchen for my two brothers and I. Here Doris would sit in a straight-backed Windsor chair in front of a glowing fire, the range shining with blacklead and the oil lamp giving a soft glow as well as extra warmth, and all was secure. Her steel needles clicked away endlessly as she knitted all Dad's socks.

Sometimes she would read us stories and if we asked her very nicely she would sing in a rather shrill but tuneful voice all the verses of 'The Campbells are coming'. I thought it was the camels with four legs that were coming. The other favourite song was 'Jesus bids us shine'.

We were very impressed when a man came to take Doris out on her half day off. This was Mac, and he had a motorbike and side-car. She was always in at 9 pm and we speculated all day as to whether he would kiss her goodnight. Excitement grew as the hour approached and we all piled into the front bedroom to get a good view. We were not disappointed so our day was complete.

Time came for Doris to make her own life and move away but my memory of her is still vivid. Sometimes when I get up from the table I hear her voice say, "Side yer chairs". Yes, Doris.' *(Janet Isaac – South Cave WI)*

▧ GROWING UP IN DUNSWELL IN THE 1950s ▧

'It was just after the war and some things were still rationed. Money was scarce so we had to make do as best as we could.

There was always a roast joint on the table each Sunday, but we children never got any. We were each given a tea-plate size Yorkshire pudding with a spoonful of syrup. By the time we had ploughed our way through it, we were too full up to eat anything else. I don't know what would have happened if we were not because no vegetables had been prepared for us, as if Mother had planned it. However, it always meant there was enough meat left over for Father on Monday. Apart from the Sunday joint, no other meat was bought. Father worked on the land and so supplied us with rabbits, hares and "stoggies". I don't know what the experts would say now but we always argued over who got the head in the rabbit pie as the brain was the tastiest part.

Our diet was supplemented with fish. The older boys caught pike in Barmston Drain, whilst we younger children caught eels in Skidby Drain. We laid a pea basket down in the water and blocked the route on either side with stones. The eels swam up and down the drain every day at the same time so we knew when to expect them. In the early evening we crouched quietly on the bank, watching them slowly approach. As soon as one swam into the basket we whipped it out of the water. We took the eel out and laid the trap down again. After a while the water settled down again and more eels cautiously swam towards us. When we had a bag full we took them home and Mother cooked them straight away.

Each Wednesday was baking day when Mother made a week's supply of pies and tarts – fruit pies from Grandma's endless supply of fresh and bottled fruit. Breakfast was a choice of bread and milk – chunks of bread soaked with boiling water and milk – or bread and dip – dripping scraped from the roasting tin, especially the brown jelly at the bottom. Each tea was always finished with our filling up with plenty of home-made bread and jam. Our diet was not healthy by today's standard but we were always sufficed – the main object of the day.

Sweets were a treat. When rhubarb was in season we were given a stick of it together with a bag of sugar to dip it in. Bread cost elevenpence a loaf so if we went to the shop we were allowed to spend the penny change on sweets. My favourites were aniseed balls – eight for a penny. I also liked penny liquorice and always chose the Catherine wheel because it lasted the longest – far longer than the pipes or twists. Gobstoppers were two for a penny and lasted a long while but you had to keep taking them out of your mouth to see what colour they had changed to. My mother banned me from buying sherbet because she said it was only coloured sugar and bad for me. She told the shopkeeper Douggie not to sell me any but I soon got round that by sending my friend Maureen into the shop for me. Penny Arrow bars came in all different flavours – liquorice, strawberry and treacle but my favourite was banana.

If you saved your pennies for a few days then you could treat yourself to a McGowan's toffee bar, a packet of Beechnut chewy or a bar of Five Boys chocolate. If you were really lucky then the arrow on the chewy machine was pointing forward and you got a free packet with your penny.

Each Sunday we were sent to Sunday school. Father was "chapel" and Mother was "church" so we were sent to both. We went to the church first, St Faith's. We always arrived before the Sunday school teacher and so we played our favourite game. We piled up the hassocks to see who could kneel on the highest stack before toppling over. The person who arrived first always "bagsed" the vicar's hassock because it was twice as thick and made a sound base on which to build.

Half-way through the service a group of us left to walk up to the Methodist chapel. Again we always arrived before the teacher so had to amuse ourselves for a while. The organ was always locked up but we soon found that if one person worked the pedals then another could put their hands up under the keyboard and play a tune.

During one particular candlelit service, I was given the job of shining a light on the music for the organist. As I glanced round at the congregation, I saw the teacher frantically jerking her head and pointing. I just assumed she had finally flipped from years of putting up with us. I tried to ignore her but the jerks became more frantic. Suddenly there was a loud bang from over by the windowsill behind me. As I ran across the room, white with shock, my teacher said, "I did try to warn you that the candle was almost burnt down to the glass dish it was standing in." To this day I am still too afraid to use glass candle holders.

A group of students at the teacher training college in Hull had the bright idea of taking our Sunday school for a while – they decided it would be good experience for them! They could not believe it when we asked them if we could be let out early to see the "Old Crocks Race". It took us a while to convince them it was genuine. The Hull to Bridlington Veteran Car Rally, as it was officially known, passed through the village each September and you could always guarantee at least one would come to a grinding, chugging halt with steam coming out from under the bonnet. It was great fun to see the ladies dressed up in their old-fashioned costumes, frantically trying to hold their bonnets on, and the gentlemen honking their horns at us and waving.

The chapel had high backed pews with doors at the ends. During prayer time we would bob down so that the students could not see us. At the end we all emerged – in different places. This totally confused them. The only person they could track was my cousin Mally because he had a clever knack of blowing puffs of steam into the cold air and it looked as if a miniature steam train was moving up and down along the pews.

During the week we had to find a different source of entertainment. We children all congregated on the playing field at the village "insti". The boys would play football and the girls would sit around making daisy chains. Sometimes we would all play Block, British Bulldogs or Eggety Budge. The latter involved the chosen person being allowed three strides, three spits, eight fairy steps, a ladder and a lob with the ball to reach as many people as possible. Anyone who was tigged three times had to run the Tunnel – everyone had to line up with their hands resting against a wall to form a tunnel. Those who had incurred three penalties had to run the length of the tunnel, being thumped on the back all the way. It sounds sadistic and probably would be banned in today's playgrounds but it was one of our favourite games – we saw it as "character building". No one chickened out of the penalty, but no one was ever hurt. I don't know if it was peculiar to our village or if it was a local or national game.

One evening we had all gathered at the playing field as usual to find a whist drive taking place in the institute. We saw our chance for a bit of fun. We wriggled under the institute and located where the people inside were sitting. Then we knocked on the wooden floor. It wasn't long before someone came out to see what the noise was. He couldn't see anything so he went back inside. We waited a few moments then knocked again. Out he came again. This went on several times until he decided it was only a dog or something. He was just about to go back inside when he spotted a lad at the corner. It was Oofah The Doofah – the poor lad who always seemed to be in the wrong place at the wrong time. He had only just arrived and knew nothing about what was happening but never got a chance to explain before he got a good telling off and a clip round the ear. He was too loyal to tell on us and fell about laughing when we emerged.

Life for my husband was just as hard in Hedon. His mother used to send him and his brothers to the railway embankment with a bucket to collect the cinders the stoker threw off the trains. One day he was shouting abuse at the driver so the fireman picked up a lump of coal and threw it at him. He soon learnt how to annoy the fireman and how to dodge the missiles and from then on they had the best fire around with real coal!

My husband and his brothers earned a reputation for their wily ways in their struggle for survival. It took him longer to pluck up the courage to go and see the vicar to have our banns read out than it did to ask me to marry him. Being naive I did not understand the problem until the vicar smiled at my husband and said it was nice to see him inside the church instead of on it!'
(Judy Wilson – Kilham WI)

Schooldays – The Best Years of Our Lives?

Long walks to school, wet clothes steaming round the fire, slates and chalk, crossed nibs and inkwells – what memories they bring back of schooldays in small village schools.

▓ First Lessons ▓

'It's Monday. I know it's Monday because I have my clean clothes on and Mrs Hill has come to do the washing. I'm going to school for the first time. I put my coat on and Mum puts the large woollen scarf round my neck, crosses it in front and ties it at the back as the wind is cold.

"Hurry back at dinner time, Jane, and I will have a rice pudding ready for you," says Mum.

"In my own dish?" I ask.

"Yes, in your own small dish."

A quick hug and a kiss at the door and I am on my own. No

Welton school pupils – all of them – in 1920. (Hazel Widd – Welton WI)

105

two brothers to walk with me, Joe and Eric have gone to another school and they told me I must have another birthday before I can go with them. Why Eric can't miss some weeks so that I can catch up with him and we can be the same age I don't know, I've asked and asked him but he says he can't do that.

The only house near us has a solid wooden fence across the yard to keep the chickens in. Don my friend lives here and his elder brother Lenny…we are both afraid of him. The dogs bark as I pass and rattle their chains. Our Peggy is never fastened up and often goes to church with us on Sundays, sleeping under Mum's feet, giving an odd snort during the sermon, making us giggle.

I catch up with other children going to school. A teacher shows us where to hang our coats. There are two rooms and we are in the smaller one at the back. Both have large glowing fires burning. I am too shy to tell the teacher that I know my letters and can read, my sisters have seen to that, but I have learned the grown up's letters. School letters are different with pictures…A ferapple, B ferbat, C fercat. Play time is fun. I am chosen for "Poor Mary sat a-weeping" but I know all the songs. Just time for one game of "Sly Fox" and it's time to go in.

When it is time to go home the others race away. They haven't far to go. As I pass the cottages some of the children are sitting on the door steps eating whole slices of bread and jam. How lucky they are. I wish they would ask me to join them. I hurry on. If I asked for bread and jam at home I would have to sit at the table and the slice would be cut up on a plate. If only I could have a whole slice in my hand. My fingers would reach from crust to crust and Mum's new "rasp" jam would be spread over the top. I would be very careful not to let it spill down my dress.

Back home Mum takes off my scarf and coat.

"Had a good morning, Jane? What have you learnt?"

"U ferumbrella," I burst out. Mum looks a bit surprised but says nothing. She only knows the grown-up letters.

Next morning something happens to spoil my walk to school for some weeks. I was just level with the fence when Lenny's head pops up over the top, making me jump. I try not to look afraid, then stones start bouncing onto the path, just missing my

Football was always popular with the boys – teams from Kilham and Welton in the 1920s. (Cecily Wilson – Kilham WI; Hazel Widd – Welton WI)

legs and I start to run. What can I do? Unless I hurt myself Mum always says, "Don't come crying to me, fight your own battles." How can I fight with someone twice as big as me? Maybe Uncle Sam would help...but he doesn't come until Christmas and that's a long way off. So I must keep this to myself, try and pass quietly and then run.

But it didn't always work. I was glad when I was kept at home with spots and I think Lenny had grown tired of waiting for me, so when I started school again I was left in peace. I had sorted my first battle out on my own! *(Janet Isaac – South Cave WI)*

▣ First Days ▣

'I remember my first day at school very clearly. It was just after Christmas in the early 1930s. My grandmother dressed me with care in long woollen stockings and brown leather gaiters as well as a very heavy navy coat and to finish off, mittens on strings and a velour hat with elastic under the chin.

The school looked rather dark with green tiling half-way up the walls. We had to stand in line with the other mothers and children to be "registered" with the headmistress, a lady called Mrs Bollum. Then we were led away to our first class which had a lovely fire in the corner with a big nursery fire guard around it. On wet days our coats were dried or warmed by hanging them over the guard.

The teacher, an angel called Miss Simpson, taught us to sew amongst all the other lessons. I remember clearly making a crepe paper dress like a bright red poppy with green leaves for the skirt. Every Monday morning we took our bank books and money to school for the Penny Bank. My book was kept in a mauve and white checked cloth bag to keep it clean. On one occasion I swopped a £1 note, that had been given as a present from a great aunt, for a half crown (2/6d) piece that a friend had, thinking in my innocence that it was more valuable as it felt heavier than the £1 note. Needless to say, my grandmother and this girl's mother went hot foot to school to see Mrs Bollum!

When it came to Christmas time each person in the class was

Kilham schoolchildren before the First World War. (Isobel Shepherdson – Stamford Bridge WI)

asked to take a carrot, bread crumbs, dried fruit etc until we had all the necessary ingredients to make a Christmas pudding. We all helped mix it and made a wish. This was cooked in a large pan on a gas ring in the classroom. On the last day of term we ate the pudding with rum sauce – delicious. I still love Christmas pudding – especially the rum sauce.' *(Brenda Falk – Elloughton cum Brough WI)*

▨ FIRES AND FEVER ▨
'Our village school has long since been closed to pupils, but still stands as a reminder of happy days.

I started school when I was five years old. I lived quite a long walk away, and on my way I used to call for my best friend, who at first hated school. She cried every day. I remember putting my arm around her and telling her everything would be alright!

The school had two rooms. The larger room was kept warm in

the winter by a big coal-burning stove, and the smaller room by a coal fire. We had two teachers and we stayed until we were eleven years old, having sat an exam called the "eleven plus". There was a large field at the back along with a playground. The toilets were outside.

We had a mid-morning break of Horlicks made with hot milk. The Horlicks was in a large catering tin which when empty we were allowed to take home. I don't know what we used it for, but it was exciting when my turn came around.

When I was seven I contracted scarlet fever. I was the only person in the village to do so. I had to go to Driffield for seven weeks to an isolation hospital, and the only visitors I had were my father and auntie. My mother was pregnant at the time so she wasn't allowed to visit. Dad and Auntie could only look at me through a glass window. When I returned to school my books had been packed in a brown paper parcel and put on top of a cupboard. I expect that was so no one else could contract the disease. All my time tables had to be rewritten into a new book, in fact I was given all new books, much to the envy of the other pupils!

My mother, who believed everything had to be really properly aired before being worn, used to put my navy blue knickers on the fireside oven door. One morning I was on my way to school when suddenly I heard her shouting, "You've forgotten to put your knickers on." Luckily, no one was around to hear her.' *(Jean Dowling – Hollym WI)*

❀ SCHOOL CLOTHES ❀

'Oh, to grow up and have a suspender belt instead of bunches of suspenders hanging from the sides of our liberty bodices!

We wore bottle green knickers which washed out to pea green in due time. Our PE shirts were named in chain stitch across our chests. Some names were stretched across 36B cup, others shrunk awaiting developments.

When clothes and shoes were rationed we had clothing coupons (after the war), but children's shoes were exempt. The

Thearne pupils at Woodmansey school in 1930. (J. Wilson – Kilham WI)

day the seniors all got their coupons Mum was quite irate that I didn't take any home. When she enquired at school they apologised and said they didn't think anybody in the Juniors would have feet so big. She insisted that mine were measured and I got my coupons. I still take size seven and a half.' *(Bunty Appleby – Nafferton WI)*

' There are mixed feelings about the clothes we wore as children. There were very cosy liberty bodices, fleecy lined, tape reinforced and fastened with rubber buttons. Very full petticoats, cotton or flannel with or without lace trimmings, and knickers, good solid sensible knickers, navy blue and fleece lined for winter, cotton and rather stiff for summer. If they had pockets, and most of them did, hankies were stored in them. No pockets and hankies had to be tucked into the elastic that was around the legs and which left red rings where it cut in. Sometimes hankies wandered.

There were no zip fasteners until the mid 1930s so garments were fastened by buttons and buttonholes or loops, by press fasteners, or by hooks and eyes. Buttonhooks were useful tools but could nip fiercely if used on shoe straps or long many-buttoned gaiters. These came over the knee, were fleece-lined and chafed your thighs if they got wet. School stockings were made of brown or black wool or lisle thread. They were itchy and wrinkled down your legs (shades of Nora Batty). Any irritable tug left holes to be darned – neatly. Holes in heels could sometimes be camouflaged by a careful dab of black ink.' *(Ella Musgrove for Fangfoss with Bolton WI)*

▨ I HATED IT ▨

'A few years after my father came back from the war, First World War of course, he got a job with Mr George Stephenson (Boss) as foreman (Gaffer) at Springdale Farm, Rudston.

We moved into Hind House and I think my mother got the worst of the bargain. She had to cook for and look after five men living in, and during harvest time there were 16 men living in the house. We had our own sitting room and staircase up to our bedrooms. We also had my mother's grandfather living with us until he died a few years later. My mother made all her own bread (two stone of flour twice a week) as well as all the other baking and meals. The grocers from Rudston, Corner's, came up to deliver goods each week. She also had to make and deliver mid-morning and mid-afternoon break, usually scones and cheese and a drink, out to the men when they were working in the fields away from the farm.

Apart from this she made all their beds, which wasn't just a straightening of duvets as it might be today, but sheets, blankets to be put straight and tucked in as well as the flock beds fluffed up. She also had the unenviable task of emptying all the chamber pots, one to each bed. We didn't have a WC but two "one-holer" outside closets, which had squares of newspaper fastened together through a hole in the corner.

Even though we had our own rooms, at night I liked to sit round the kitchen fire with its large oven at one side and boiler at the other, clipped rug in front of the hearth and listen to the men talking. Every now and again I would hear one whisper, "Mind what you say, young lugs are listening," or, "Bairn's with us."

I eventually had to go to school in Rudston three miles away, which I hated. I had always been on my own at the farm and it was awful to be amongst all these children. The teachers Miss Moss and Miss Corner were very kind but I still hated it. At dinner time I went into the village to my mother's aunt's to have my dinner. This I was a little afraid of as this aunt had a deaf and dumb son, Tom, who was the village cobbler. He was always very good to me as my mother had taken the trouble to learn sign language and so was able to communicate with him, but when frustrated he had been known to chase his mother round the kitchen table with a carving knife. Thankfully he never caught her and I don't know if he would have done anything if he had!

In the winter we were always snowed in at the farm and this I really enjoyed for two reasons. Firstly because I loved playing in the snow, clearing paths etc, but mainly because I couldn't get through to go to school. When at school, one of our "things" was to go across the road at playtime to the Monolith because we had been told, "If you prick it with a pin it will bleed." We all tried many times but never managed to get the pin to go in!

On my way home from school in the summer I used to take hours as I would stop and sit on the grassy banks at the side of the road making daisy chains, pipes with hips and hawthorn spikes, or whistles made from bad man's oatmeal stems. I was always a keen wild flower girl. My mother never worried about how long I took to get home. It never entered my head I would not be safe.' *(Edith Hopkinson – Sutton on Hull WI)*

▩ SCHOOL TRANSPORT ▩

'I live in Driffield and I went to school in Bridlington at nine years old. I went in a two carriage steam train from Malton called the "Malton Dodger". It was filled mostly with girls going to the High School but it wasn't particularly timed for our purpose. It left Driffield at 7.50 am and arrived in Bridlington at 8.20 am so we had a leisurely stroll to school. Homecoming, our train was an express from Scarborough (full of buckets and spades in the summer) which left Bridlington at 5.15 pm.

To prevent us "wandering off" or anything like that we were expected to do prep in a room at school, known as the Driffield Train Prep Room. I arrived home at 6 pm and I immediately sat down to my hot meal during which I discussed anything with my parents as it was the only time I had to speak with them during the week. I then went to do my homework, have a bath and perhaps get things ready for the next day. I usually fell into bed exhausted by 10 pm to 10.15 pm – and people say to me, "Didn't you even belong to the Guides?"

Some homework was done on the Malton Dodger and pens, gloves, train passes etc were often left on the ledges. The railway company always charged our parents for the items left – the cost of travelling to Malton and back. My Mum spent a fortune paying for my fountain pen and my gloves to do that journey.

We were very naughty on the trains. As each coach was self contained we were not bothered by a conductor. Our favourite trick was to climb on the luggage rack so when the train stopped at the many villages, passengers got into our compartment thinking it was empty! Then we all jumped down.' *(Bunty Appleby – Nafferton WI)*

▨ On the Whole ▨

'On the whole I enjoyed my school days, starting off in the kindergarten at Bridlington High School for Girls. Miss Norfolk and Miss Stanger were our teachers. One thing which sticks in my mind was the lesson we had outdoors in the rose garden outside the headmistress's study. Here we observed a sun dial and learnt how to "read" it and its uses through antiquity. We collected dandelion heads, made a circle and used them to make the "time" shadow. That memory and knowledge has stayed with me for 70 odd years.

As we grew older we progressed to the "big" school and I struggled with arithmetic and English. Every year I managed to get bronchitis near my birthday in October and spent weeks in

Bridlington High School pupils in 1932. (Shirley Franklin – Driffield WI)

Playing netball on Bridlington beach in the 1930s. (Shirley Franklin – Driffield WI)

bed, missing lessons which were so important for the early understanding of those two subjects, which blight me to this day! However, one year I enjoyed immensely was 1935. To celebrate the Silver Jubilee of King George V and Queen Mary, the school had a sports day, a presentation of commemorative mugs and a huge tableau of school girls from all forms, in white blouses and navy knickers, forming the dates 1910-1935 with suitable patriotic music.

Round about 1935 my brother Bob, who was a day boy at Marton Hall School, caught mumps so we four girls, aged between eleven and five years, were put into quarantine and kept away from school. So that we were kept busy, a project was suggested by the teachers in the kindergarten to make a complete doll's cot. With the help of our Nanny, and Nanny Help, we lined a big box, padded it, made a mattress, pillows with slips, sheets and blankets topped with an eiderdown and gave it to the Infants class to play with. We also had "homework", of course; and we never caught mumps! That winter we all caught whooping cough, what a palaver, a special lamp burnt camphor giving off a soothing aroma to relieve the coughing, and later we all caught measles! Being a member of a large family and very close in ages, if one got an infection it usually passed on to the others.

Later I was at Devonshire House School, a small private school which my father thought would help my schooling. It was run by two elderly spinsters called the Misses Duggleby. One taught music and divinity and the other one history and English literature, and French. One other lady, Miss Allan, taught us maths and geography and saw to the "energetic" side of the school, she being much younger than the Misses Duggleby.

Our school room was a large wooden shed with an open Ideal boiler stove to heat it, lovely for those nearest but cold for those pupils further back. The "room" was divided by curtains on runners so that several times a week more than one or two classes were being taught in that one big room. It made one learn to concentrate!

Our games area was behind the Palace Cinema, a small grassy area, ideal for exercises but not for games which we transferred to the sands. We played netball on the beach when the tide was out.' *(Shirley Franklin – Driffield WI)*

THE WORLD OF WORK

On the Land

Farming seemed hardly to have changed over the century, until the advent of mechanisation forced the working horse from the land. It was often a hard life but one which gave great satisfaction to many of those who followed it.

▣ Farming at Buttercrambe ▣

'My first introduction to the work of harvesting was as a schoolgirl, driving carts after school and on Saturdays. Taking the empty cart back to the field was a doddle. With long enough reins I could sit in the cart and drive in comfort, or to sit side saddle with my feet on the shafts was quite easy. The journey from field to stackyard was another ball game entirely. The field we would be working in would probably be down some rough old cart track and with this rattling the cart and making it go 'umpity humpity bump' the horse would end up going like hell and I would have to run to try to keep up with it. Perhaps it was the weight of the load or the rough terrain that would make the horse dig its toes in and go like the wind, but I had to run to keep up. Coming to a rough rutted patch the load would bounce and sway like a boat in a force eight gale. You might drop a few sheaves but you didn't worry unless the whole load "pigged". If you hit an extra big pot hole and all the sheaves and corn skelled off, they would say "the load's pigged". Then I would have to run back and shout for help and just hope that the horse didn't get down in its traces or something. The only advice I had was that if by some mischance the horse stumbled and fell I must immediately sit on its head and shout and holler at the top of my voice until help arrived. With any luck I would get most of the load delivered to the stackyard.

A while later my next job was "picking on the stack". A team of three usually worked there. No 1, on the cart, was teeming

Horse teams at Riplingham Farm. (John Harrison – Bainton)

(unloading). No 2 was picking and tossing the sheaf to the stacker. No 3 – this was a knack in itself. A flick of the wrist to turn the sheaf in midair to present it to the stacker in the correct position. Working to a steady rhythm the stack grew apace. It always fascinated me being on the stack. It moved like something alive. Rather like trying to walk on the Bouncy Castle that children love so much today. Getting up higher as the stack is built up layer by layer, a new vista opened as you could see over the roof tops and into the tops of trees. "Ho! so that's where my kite finally landed – in the guttering between the fold yard and the stables." "That tennis ball must have been there for years!"

As the stack was nearing completion and the shaping of the eaves continued I had to stay in one position – the picking hole, in glorious isolation. Held prisoner there until the last sheaf was fixed, while the "roof" of the stack was being built up all around. No room to do anything else but gather the sheaf and pass it on to the stacker. If there was a lull between carts I would sit down in a world of my own. The rustle of the settling corn and the almost tangible buzz of myriads of insects making it seem that I was in Fairy Land. Then it was back to earth – "I can't find a long ladder. You'll have to come down this little one into the cart and then jump". Finally it was indoors to late tea or supper. Tangy plum pie and cream made a fitting end to a busy day.

On farms in those days you would have threshing days. The engine men would bring their engines to you the night before and then set up all the threshing machine, ready for starting at six or seven o'clock in the morning. There were usually at least three engine men and they would all stay for their teas the night before. Next morning they would come in for their breakfast and then the threshing would start. Thee would be anything from ten to 15 men working the threshing machine and our job also included getting their lunch and 'llowance.

The 'llowance was their afternoon drinks – a bucket full of coffee plus a great big apple pie or a great big hunk of scone and cheese. The coffee would be made in a bucket. Four or five tablespoons of coffee, pour boiling water on and stir it up. Then chuck a jug of milk in and a wallop of sugar. We would take it to them either in a bucket or a couple of great big milk cans and we would serve it with a tin jug and all the old pint mugs that we could find.

The men would be hired for the day to do jobs such as moving the chaff, carrying the corn, feeding the machine, cutting the bands and doing all the jobs that were necessary. The wages at the time I am thinking of would probably be about five bob a day for a day's threshing and that would be big money. Anybody in labouring in those days would get paid at the end of the month or the end of their time and if they wanted any money beforehand they would go to the boss and have a sub which was duly accounted for and docked off their money. George had evidently heard a saying from the men about this, because he came out with it the other day, "I think I'll just go t'boss and sub a pund and then go and have a pissup!" Some men would do what you would call tramp threshing, following the machine from farm to farm, walking behind it unless they had a bike or something. The farms would be two or three miles distance, although up on the wolds they could be four or five. There were not many days that we had to hire in extra labourers but I remember there was often a group of Irishmen who would come round seeking work. There were probably quite a few that would come regularly and you would get to know them.

Dad was a tenant farmer. The farm was owned by Darley Estates which was based at Alby Park, a big redbrick house on a hill near Buttercrambe. In the park there were deer. We never got invited up to the house but my dad went up every year for the puppy walk. Up at Birdsall were the hunt kennels and they used to billet out the young puppies on the farmers to grow up and then when they were a certain age they were called back to the kennels to train. That was called puppy walking and we always had one or two of these foxhounds. We would keep them for so long and then there would be this annual bunfight, feast and a show when they judged these puppies. They gave prizes for the best bitch and the best dog or the best pair and then they had a nice meal and a nice afternoon's "kowtowing" around.

The economics of farming were always up and down. One period we would be quite well off and then farming got that it was pretty bad times – it got that you spent so much an acre on seed and labouring and what have you and you would be lucky if you got about a quarter of it back on your produce. Farmers lived on their losses and kept hoping. In the 1920s and 1930s especially, money was a scarce commodity, but we lived off the land and never went hungry. In those days farmers were notoriously poor gardeners. Dad was erratic in that respect. Some seasons we had everything; early lettuce, radishes, onions, peas, beans – runner, dwarf and broad, celery, cabbages, cauliflower and sprouts. Other times vegetables were not so plentiful, depending no doubt on how farm work progressed.

One year I remember in particular Mother was chivying, "When are you going to get that garden dug?" "Oh, don't worry," he replied. "I'll have it done." The next I knew was while I was doing my bedroom I heard such a commotion below in the garden. "Whoa. Gee up. Get back you stupid old…!" Dad was performing with a plough, drawn by the youngest, flightiest horse we had, one barely broken in! The soil was getting turned over at a fair rate of knots. Not stopping for the box hedge which marked the path down the middle of the garden. The aforesaid box hedge was now gapped like a set of broken teeth with half of them missing. The rhubarb patch nearly vanished and the gooseberry bushes had to look out. Never a dull moment!

All the children worked on the farm with never a regular wage. Fed and clothed, we had to scrape up what we could for pocket money. Snickling rabbits, shooting wood pigeons, buy an old sow for breeding and sell off the litter at eight weeks old, buy sex linked pullets or cockerels, dress the cockerels and sell, keep pullets for egg laying. Lots of farms were worked on that system. Family worked.' *(Daisy Naylor – Stamford Bridge WI)*

▓ FARM LIFE AT COTTINGHAM ▓

'I was born in 1921 in a cottage in Northgate that had been one of the old "tofts and crofts" of Cottingham. My forebears had lived in Cottingham at least since 1739 when one of my mother's ancestors was an overseer of the poor, and many of them were either market gardeners or small cow keepers. The cottage was very primitive, no electricity and gas light downstairs only, and cold water taps outside. The only sanitation (until the 1930s) was an earth closet which was situated about 100 yards away and drained into the mill beck which ran near the cottage.

In my father's time we kept upwards of 20 cows, and two horses. The milk was delivered locally, my mother made butter and curd and kept poultry and we usually kept some pigs. We had one farm worker, who worked for us from age 13 (when he took the labour exam to leave school early) until he died at the age of 55 (c1960). He described himself as a "horseman", but much of his time was spent working with the cows. He worked long hours with little time off, and he once decided he would leave. He went to Beverley hiring and took the "fest" shilling from another farmer – then thought better of it and gave the "fest" back and stayed on. He was a good ploughman, and loved his horses Bonny and Peggy, later Violet.

Harnessed up on a wolds farm at Thwing. (Isobel Shepherdson – Stamford Bridge WI)

We had a stationary engine that was used for powering the chaff (choppy) cutter, and for the turnip and worzel pulper. We had slabs of cotton and linseed cake delivered from Skidby Mill and it was crushed for the cows in a hand operated machine. We had an orchard with many old varieties of fruit trees: apples – Annie Elizabeth, Lane's Prince Albert, Fillingham, Strawberry Pippin, Green Balsam etc; William and Hazel or Hessle pears; damson – Black Diamond and Golden Drop; and Victoria plums. The cottage, land and orchard was bordered by a beck, formerly the stream that worked the North Mill (water and windmill, demolished about 1900) and in my time it had newts, frogs and occasionally eels. There were moorhens and kingfishers – and we kept Aylesbury and Khaki Campbell ducks. The beck had decreased in size when the pumping station for the Hull Waterworks began in 1890 and is now culverted.

Our cows were pastured about one and a half miles away, in Park Lane and had to be driven down the streets – causing fun and games after the winter's incarceration in the cowhouses in Northgate. They were milked outside, and the milk brought back in a churn in the "light" cart; this was a high cart with large iron-shod wheels. In school holidays it was a treat for me to go to help "fetch the cows up" and have a ride in the cart. In the fields there were an abundance of wild flowers, wild orchids, cowslips, ox-eye daisies, yellow rattle, ladies' slipper and also skylarks nesting (1920s).

Three things I remember – we always called the living room of the cottage the "house". "Put it in the house", meant "take it into the living room" not just the house itself.

Farm workers always rode their work horses side saddle, not astride, often hanging their jackets on the "haimes" on the horse collar.

The horses were turned when they were ploughing by the words "Gee" and "Whoave" meaning to left and right.' *(Eileen Green – Cottingham WI)*

'I left school at 14 in 1939 and went straight on to a farm to be in charge of six horses. I was the only live-in lad on that farm at that time. The day went something like this:

5 am	got up; attended to horses
6.30 am	breakfast
7 am	out to fields
12 noon	dinner; fed horses
1 pm	back to work
5 pm	finish work; attended to horses
6 pm	tea
After tea	with horses (until about 7 or 7.30 pm)

I was paid £24 a year, plus food. It was a seven-day a week job, 52 weeks a year, but in my second year I got Sunday afternoon off. When I was 16 I was paid £36 a year, plus food. It was hard work and hard conditions. There were some 100 acre fields and, after harvest, when you were horse-raking and if it was a fog you never saw other chaps working the same field all day.

In the winter of 1947 we had to walk to work and back (five miles) every day for seven weeks. The snow was ten feet high. Before that, 1941 was a long winter as well. The foreman thought we were in danger of running out of meat and he sent me to Market Weighton (one mile on foot and then bus) to bring back a stone of beef.

There was a clear order of procedure on farms among workers. When we had a wash the towel was first used by the shepherd, then the waggoner, then third lad (me), then fourth lad if there was one. I can only remember the towel being very wet when I got it. We were warm enough when we were able to go to the saddle house where there was a fire and a dart board.

During the Second World War we had prisoners of war helping on the farms and, of course, land girls. I married one of them (Doris Berriman) and we spent happy years on East Riding farms. The land girls were willing workers, but not always as knowledgeable as they might have been. Two of them were very pleased that they had managed to hitch a horse up to a cart – except the cart had no wheels.

The 'third lad' with working horses. (Isobel Shepherdson – Stamford Bridge WI)

We were quite close neighbours to a gamekeeper on a farm at Middleton-on-the-Wolds. He lived in a wooden place built on stilts. Gamekeepers were not the most popular men, because their job was to protect game for the estate owners when some of their neighbours might be the poachers!

We had a Manx cat at one time. It was one of eight and over a two-week period he delivered on to our back doorstep game bird feathers and the straps which the gamekeeper used in spring-time to restrict the birds' flight. Tommy Tennant, the keeper, said he was worried about the birds he was losing. My wife didn't say anything, but she suspected he knew it was our cat. Anyway, the cat disappeared after a short while.

The fiercest cat I ever remember was a black one. No dog could best her! She got caught in one of the gin traps which keepers used to put in strategic places. She managed to pull out the stake which the keepers used to mark the trap's position, but she had broken her shoulder. The keeper let her out and she managed to get to a good, old tree and pulled her shoulder back by clawing down the bark with so much strength as she could muster. Her claw was never right, but she survived.' *(John Harrison, of Bainton)*

◻ BYGONE DAYS ◻

'There are memories of the bygone days on farms when lunches or "llowances" were taken out to the men in the fields. One lady remembers using a pram to carry them out because her grandmother had 22 men to provide for. It was customary for single men to live in at the foreman's house. There were as a rule two staircases, one going up to the large room generally over the kitchen, and all the men slept together in the one room.

The men used to have a large wooden box containing their clothes and personal possessions which they took with them from farm to farm as they moved about. They were generally hired for one year at a time and if they weren't asked to stay, they moved on. There was a strict "pecking order", beginning with the foreman and ending with the lad at the lower end, with the

Sheep shearing at Kilham. (Isobel Shepherdson – Stamford Bridge WI)

waggoner and thoddie etc fitted in between.

A fresh pie at meal times was only ever started when the foreman decided it should be. There was a way of cutting it at an angle, not quite reaching the centre, that left a crustless piece in the centre and that was enjoyed by the foreman.' *(Barbara Moorcroft – Rudston WI)*

'In the 1930s I spent a lot of time at Hood Hill Farm where my friend Vera lived. Life was wonderful in those days, with always something exciting to do and places to explore. In the harvest season however we had to do our bit in the corn fields, stooking the sheaves of corn. We didn't like it as the stubble scratched our legs and the sheaves cut into our arms and if we didn't stook the sheaves correctly we were told off. We never had time to be bored though.

I continued helping on the farm in the early years of the war, when soldiers from the nearby army base came to help with the harvest. They went into the fields to stook while we ladies had to produce refreshment. We were allowed extra rations and sandwiches and huge containers of tea were taken out to the fields twice a day. When it got to the last strip to be harvested the farmer and local gamekeeper were there with their guns. In the end the rabbits had to run for it and many were shot, their bodies loaded into the back of an old van. Back at the farm they were skinned and gutted and they provided the meat for our rabbit stew. Vegetables were obtained from a small garden at the back of the farm and the soldiers enjoyed a very tasty home-cooked meal.' *(Betsy Wood – Sewerby WI)*

▨ THRESHING DAY ▨

'Childhood memories come flooding back at the mention of threshing day.

My father was a tenant farmer when I was young, and to me threshing day was a very special occasion. My day started earlier than usual, I awoke to the smell of bacon and eggs cooking. The owners of the threshing machine came to breakfast, and us

Threshing day. (Jean Dowling – Hollym WI)

children had to wait for our meal until they had finished.

The threshing team consisted of local men, all with their own special jobs to do. Very often several of the men were brothers and uncles of the same family. Soon the hum of the engine could be heard, and the stackyard was a hive of activity. The sheaves of corn were fed into the machine, being forked up from the stack harvested in the autumn. The corn fell into waiting bags, weighing 16 stone, and was carried up granary steps and emptied onto the floor. One man had to carry chaff in a large sheet, a very dusty job.

Meanwhile, my mother was kept busy all day. The morning lunch for the men consisted of scones baked in a side oven, and a large bucket of strong tea, drunk from pint mugs. At dinner time the owners of the threshing machine sat down to dinner. I could never understand why they didn't go home to eat, they only lived down the village! Afternoon lunch was apple pie, freshly baked again by my mother, with another bucket of tea.

Towards the end of the day the mice who had lived in the stack soon found themselves homeless, and made a run for it. Local dogs and cats had a busy time trying to catch them. Quite a few escaped, even though a net was placed around the stack to try and stop them.

One funny, but true story, sticks in my mind. The owner was cutting the bands of the sheaves to feed them into the machine when he gave a sneeze and his false teeth shot out of his mouth and disappeared. He shouted down to the man in charge of the corn to look out for them. Sad to say they were never found!

If I close my eyes I can still see and smell this wonderful (to me), very happy day.' *(Jean Dowling – Hollym WI)*

OTHER WAYS WE MADE A LIVING

There were, of course, many other ways we made a living and those recorded here can only be a small proportion of the whole – from domestic service to mole catching and climming!

▣ SCHOOL DAYS AS A YOUNG TEACHER ▣

'When I was on my first school practice, done then towards the end of the first term in college, I was in a slum school in a very poor area in Halifax. In my class I had twin girls. One day I was cross with one of the twins and the other immediately picked up her inkwell and threw it at me. She was a good shot too.

At the end of that same practice I discovered tiny pimples appearing between my fingers which were very itchy. It was only about two or three days before the end of term, so I didn't go to Matron to report. I waited until I went home, to be dragged immediately by my mother to the GP who exclaimed, "Good God, where have you been?" Well, the dreaded verdict was scabies, and the treatment, oh dear, what a calamity! Bath in front of the farm kitchen fire in a long zinc bath filled with hot water from the electric copper, quite a luxury in those days, scrub all the infected area, step out, sit naked on a stool and dry naturally, without a towel, in front of the fire, then smear sulphur ointment all over, this to be done every four hours. After a week, persevering with this treatment, the rash had spread all over me and was getting worse, so back to the doctor I went. The verdict – I was allergic to sulphur, so I had to carry on with the same treatment but smear with boracic ointment instead. The consequence was I had got rid of the dreaded disease by Christmas.

Another recollection is of when the River Ouse burst its banks in 1947 and all the countryside round about was flooded to a depth of ten bricks on the school house wall. I was teaching at Barlby at the time, and apart from the headmaster, who lived in the school house, was the only teacher living east of the river and the only one able to get there by a mixture of Shanks's pony, bicycle, rail and "duck", an amphibious vehicle belonging to the army. We were about a week ladling mud out of the classrooms and in the midst of it the Chief Education Officer turned up to see how the evacuation was going on. He never forgot it and often referred to it in later years. The result of that flood – we had to dry all the books in the sunshine and use them again. I have books, which I read to my grandchildren today, which were discoloured by the flood water. It's a wonder we didn't all get typhoid!' *(H.M. Garner – Atwick WI)*

▣ THE TELEPHONE COMES TO HEDON ▣

'My grandmother, Mrs Jessie Train, was the first caretaker operator at the Hedon Telephone Exchange. I am not sure of the date of her arrival, but in 1916, when I was born in Hull, my mother pushed me in my pram to visit, so it was before that year.

The small switchboard was in the corner of the sitting room, together with all the usual sitting room furniture. My grandmother's daughter Ida was the daytime operator. The house was in Souttergate, and is now the dentist's surgery. It consisted of a shop, which was empty, and there was a public call box just inside the door.

I spent my holidays with my grandmother, and one of my earliest recollections was climbing up to the switchboard chair and pulling out all the plugs. My grandmother quickly reconnected Colonel White, remembering to whom he was speaking (as he could be a bit sharp) and left everyone else to ring back while she dealt with me suitably.

In the 1930s a purpose-built telephone exchange was built at the top of Ketwell Lane, and my grandmother moved in (this has since been pulled down). After a few years, she retired, and my mother (Mrs Ellen Marshall) took over and we moved from Hull. Thus my first address in Hedon was Telephone Exchange, West Lane.

There was a switchroom with a double board much bigger than the old one, as by now there were more people with phones in Hedon and district. We had a bell on the landing and when people called in the night my mother had to come downstairs, connect them and wait until the caller had finished to disconnect them. The Club House at the Aerodrome was on our board and when the "bright young things" who were into flying at its beginning were in there, they frequently had my mother getting up in the night when they made a long call. When a trunk call was made from the call box just inside the front door the person had to come into the switch room to pay. My mother entered it in a book and took the money.

With the coming of automatic phones my mother had no job and we had nowhere to live.' *(Kitty Ingram – Hedon WI)*

▨ THE MOLE CATCHER ▨

'Each day in springtime about 35 years ago, when I was on my way to serve the children's lunch in the village school, I always met Codge the Moley, as he was known.

Codge was an old countryman with a rosy complexion, snow white hair showing beneath his cap and a well groomed moustache. He was clad in a tweed jacket, corduroy trousers, spats and well polished black boots.

Preparing turnips for the sheep on a wolds farm. (Margaret Parker – Kilham WI)

He was on his way to his mole traps. On his back he carried a canvas bag with a small spade protruding. The spade would be used for digging down to the mole runs. By his side, walking to heel was his small white terrier. Their pace never varied.

Codge was a man of few words. As I approached the road junction I could smell his tobacco. I bade him good morning and passed remarks about the weather. His reply was always the same two words: "Mornin' Missus." He never stopped. With a puff of his pipe, Codge and his dog went on their way.' *(Marie Grice – Bainton WI)*

⊞ CLIMMING ON BEMPTON CLIFFS ⊞

'Fowling rights on the cliffs were held in the 16th century by William Strickland and in the 17th and 18th centuries by trustees of the Ringley charity. In the 19th century the right to gather eggs from the cliffs was that of the farmers tenanting/owning the lands adjacent to the cliffs. The procedure of collecting eggs by descending the cliffs on a rope was known as 'climming'. Climmers formed into gangs and each had their own area of cliff. Each year some parts of the cliffs were left untouched to ensure a permanent supply of new birds. The climming season was from May to early July.

My father Alfred Corner was recruited in 1948 by Bob Artley who was an old hand climmer. Bob formed his own four man team which also included Bill Prince and Arthur Edmunds all of whom were novices. Fancy trusting your life down a 400 ft cliff into the hands of three complete novices. Bob Artley had been climming for many years with other teams and had rented an area of the cliffs called Jubilee point from Mr Harold Walker. These cliffs were in the field adjacent to the public lane up to the cliffs. When climming was in progress the farmer used to charge visitors 2d to enter the field to watch the climmers, he also charged the climmers in eggs for the privilege to farm his cliff face. The team were also paid in eggs. Dad took his to Woodys shop on Hilderthorpe Road and was paid 2d per egg. Mr Wood then sold the eggs to visitors coming off the train passing along Hilderthorpe Road at 6d each. In addition egg collectors came from all over the world to buy the eggs from the cliff tops as no two guillemot eggs have the same markings.

Dad went up to the cliffs from the village in his Morris 8 car, (a bit bigger than an Austin 7) which had a 6 volt battery, and when you got out of the car the lights were no more use than a torch. Some climmers worked into the late evenings, but Dad usually worked during the day and he did this until the practice was banned in 1954. Bob Artley was lowered over the cliff face on the main winch rope fixed to the winch and held around the anchorman's (my father) waist. Bob was suspended over the 400 ft high cliff face in a primitive harness wearing a miner's helmet which protected him from loose debris falling from above. He had a hand rope which was fastened to a peg on the top of the cliff and this was used to signal his team, he would give two pulls on the hand rope which meant 'lower away'.

Dad remembers having a few 'hairy' moments. He had to make footholds in the clifftop for his heels to provide leverage

Climmers on Bempton Cliffs in 1948. (Elizabeth Watts – Bempton WI)

when hauling up the climmer. One day half way through the exercise the holes began to crumble and Dad started to slide towards the cliff edge. He shouted to the winch men who cottoned on as to what was happening and jumped on top of Dad to hold him down. After reassembling their resources they were able to regroup and then complete pulling up poor old Bob.

Another such tale was when Bob was well down the cliff face and decided he wanted more rope. Instead of pulling twice on the hand rope he had a habit of bouncing up and down in his harness. Unfortunately he'd got all the rope off the winch, there was none left and every time he bounced in the harness he pulled the anchorman out of his footholds. The winch, the winch men and the anchorman were in danger of being pulled over the top of the cliff at every bounce. They were all hanging on for grim death and no doubt the air was resounding not only with the screams of the seagulls.

My mother remembers walking along the cliff tops with a gang of climmers when they came across a couple of boys aged 10 and 12 who had a rope with them which was tied around the waist of one of the boys who was leaning over the edge of the cliffs gathering eggs whilst his brother hung onto the other end of the rope for all he was worth. Needless to say when they were spotted they scarpered pretty quickly. They were John and William Waines and in later years they became famous in their own right as the Waines Special Cliff Party with their other brother Richard and Donald Bowen who worked for them making up the four man team. The Waines brothers and Richard's son, Simon, still climb the cliffs today but as the Flamborough Rescue Coast guards.

Climmers also took eggs from the common gulls who are predators of the smaller rarer birds, this was to keep the numbers under control. The eggs gathered were sold to collectors and the less rare eggs were sold for eating. They taste not unlike a goose egg, however they have a much fishier flavour. Dad says that if you throw something over the cliff face all the birds fly off screaming except the gulls who fly in fast and steal the eggs from the unprotected nests. They bring the eggs to the cliff top and break them, gobble up the yolk but because of the shape of their beaks leave much of the delicacy behind to be scavenged by the jackdaws who swoop down and devour the residue. The climmers with their great experience could also predict imminent rock falls and regularly cleared loose rocks from the cliff face.' *(Elizabeth Watts – Bempton WI)*

▦ NURSING TRAINING IN THE 1940s ▦

'I started my Nursing Training at the Victoria Children's Hospital, to become a Registered Children's Nurse, in 1941.

In 1942 part of the hospital was evacuated to the country, about twelve miles outside the city, to a beautiful country house in delightful grounds. I would like to recall some of the happenings.

I was sent out with another nurse and a Sister Tutor to prepare the nurses' quarters and look into our social life-to-be!

I discovered there were "village hops" on a regular basis in the village hall – 8 pm to midnight. Our limits were to be in by 10 pm and no going out after duty.

However, we discovered in our quarters a landing window leading out to a sloping hillside in the garden and we could escape to the village hall and enjoyed many a good night. The village hops became the highlight of our social life. Never a shortage of partners – the Army being in one village and the Air Force in another nearby. I think Matron and her team turned a blind eye and, possibly, would have liked to join us.

On our weekly day off we usually went home to Hull. In the next village was a fish and chip shop – only fried on certain nights. We got off the bus early and collected fish and chips for our friends. These we delivered to various bedrooms. Of course, fish and chips were not allowed in the hospital. I was once making my last delivery and came face to face along the corridor with Matron. Ordered to the office the next morning, I was told in no uncertain terms it must never happen again and there was always bread and dripping in the kitchen if we were hungry. This seemed a poor substitute.

Night duty was something else. We slept during the day in converted cow sheds and some cottages in the grounds. No running water and a privy for our toilet, but we did have a lovely coal fire in our main room. However, the coal was delivered and, unfortunately, it went in the wrong hole and Night Sister arrived back from her visit to the privy with a very black bottom. We made sure this never happened again.

Our suppers in the night were eaten around a lovely coal fire in the drawing room and we always had company – the four-legged variety with long tails – our friends the mice. We curled our legs on to chairs and wrapped our uniform dresses around.

After all this, it was an improvised hospital and we did have patients who played their part, most of them with chronic illness. The Medical Ward was all oak panelled and one little boy with a serious heart problem climbed on to the wall above the mantel shelf and gave us an almost daily rendering of "Amapoula – I'm a pretty little poppy". Although this was very much discouraged he always managed his daily concert.

I did manage to complete my training and then moved on to further training in London.' *(Ivy Richardson – Willerby & Kirkella WI)*

◩ TROUBLE AT T'MILL ◩

'In the Thirties the woollen mills had different buildings for different processes, because they had different needs. The fleeces were taken to the top of the mill where they could have roof lights to see the different qualities of wool more easily. This staggering of the work meant too that the firm could get better rates of insurance, and, as fire risks were high, it was better to have several small buildings – except for a big firm like Lister's which made the best velvet by a secret process and wanted to have keen surveillance at all times.

My father worked at Jimmy's spinning mill. He used to tell me all sorts of tales about what happened at the mill, but the story I liked best was about the young girls who worked in the spinning sheds. The young boys who came straight from school were responsible for seeing that the girls always had plenty of full bobbins so they could keep working. They were paid by the number of bobbins they emptied, so if the boys were playing marbles instead of "bobbin ligging" there was trouble. If they fell out, or if two of the girls fell out, my father used to make them stop the machines and the two had to stand in the aisle, linking their little fingers and say, "In pin, we are in." They always said it because they could not resume work until they did. Occasionally I was allowed to go into the shed and I always hoped to see one of these reconciliation sessions, but I was never so lucky.

The firm spun knitting wool for Paton and Baldwin, which was a great joy. We were always glad when a new order came in, especially a nice colour, because they always made extra yarn in case the conditioning did not weigh as much as usual. This happened more in the summer when the yarn dried out too quickly and it would have been very difficult to dye more that was an exact match. When the order had been despatched and acknowledged, the spare was sold to the workers. It was two shillings for half a pound of two ply, and half a crown for half a pound of three ply. They never made four ply, much less double knitting because only lazy women knitted wool as thick as that!

Father got a friend to show me round a weaving shed. These were mainly on the ground floor since the looms were so heavy. Outside you could hear the noise, and my guide said, "Just watch out for the picking sticks, as I shall not be able to warn you inside, you wouldn't hear." The picking stick was a stick about twelve inches long attached to the loom at one end by the drive and at the other by a leather thong. The stick sent the shuttle across the loom and the thong pulled it back. There was another at the other end to send the shuttle back. They were driven by the big steam engine and gave a very nasty blow if they hit you. The noise was horrendous. No one spoke in the weaving shed until the engine stopped for breakfast or dinner but all the weavers were experts at mime, lip reading and mouthing words, and they could talk across the shed without a sound.

After the war I was invited to a modern weaving shed and could not believe the changes. It was spotlessly clean and so quiet. There was no Puffing Billy in the cellar, but all the looms were connected individually to the mains electricity and each had its own switch. You could hear and enjoy *Workers Playtime* in comfort. Instead of harding aprons, the weavers were in pale cotton frocks. It was a revelation, much appreciated by weavers and the firm alike. Any loom could run alone or the whole shed ran together if trade was good. If the designer was not certain about a new pattern, he could go in when the girls had finished and weave the pattern to check. It also meant that the girls could work flexitime as they did not have to wait for the engine, and management were glad because they did not have to keep the boiler in all night or at weekends, they could just switch on as and when it suited them.' *(Hilda Jackson – Snaith WI)*

▣ In Service ▣

'I left North Cliffe school when I was 14, at Easter time. My mother was already working at a farm in South Cliffe. She used to go every Monday to do the washing and ironing for 2/6d. I was hired out on this farm for 4/6d a week (paid annually).

I never had to go to any hirings because I always had a job to go to before I left. The hirings were held once a year at Martinmas (23rd November) in various market towns – Driffield, Market Weighton and so on. Deals were done in the streets and in pubs. Lads from Hull would come to some of these hirings, especially those near to the city.

It wasn't an easy way to make a living! The day started at 5.30 am and stretched through to night fall. At my first job I had every other Wednesday afternoon off when I used to walk to Market Weighton, which was three miles away.

My first morning job was cleaning and black leading the kitchen grate. A big job was scalding out and cleaning the milking things – churns, separators, etc. The red-brick kitchen floor had to be scrubbed with a strong soda solution – no rubber gloves – as did the stone floors in the sleeping quarters. The only floor coverings were corn bags round the beds.

All this washing and scrubbing played havoc with your hands, especially in winter time. I rubbed "Snowfire" ointment on my hands at night and then wore cotton gloves which my mother gave to me to keep the grease off the sheets. Oh, those sheets! They were so rough and the blankets were no better. I can't bear blankets even to this day.

Friday afternoons we had to scrub the earth closet clean and then cut up newspapers to serve as toilet paper. Another cutting up job was of material to be used in making clip rugs. The tool for making the rugs was often just a wooden peg pared down to shape.

On one farm at North Cave they ran a coal business as well as a milk round. I had to deliver milk from one gallon can into people's jugs door-to-door. I also delivered butter, cream and eggs. Collecting these eggs gave me many a dreary walk round hedges, in stack yards – wherever these "free range" hens

Alice Walker, aged 25, in service at Cliffe Dale Farm, Hotham. (Alice Fallowfield – Holme on Spalding Moor WI)

decided to lay their eggs! I would try to get these delivery duties to let me off from the Sunday morning Epsom salts dosing! But I wasn't often successful.

Saturday night was bath night. This meant heating the wash house boiler and bringing out the zinc bath in front of the fire. The family followed the same routine on Friday nights.

I can remember going to the picture house in Market Weighton – Jack and Rosie Garforth's Picture House – 6d a time. We had to go to the matinee because we had to be in by nine o'clock on Saturday nights.

Two things made me feel very smart! One was a velvet (or, perhaps it was velveteen) dress made for me by Edith Davies for 10/-. The other was having my first perm when I was 17 years old. My hair was straight as pump water and the 10/- Eugene perm lasted a year!' *(Alice Fallowfield – Holme-on-Spalding Moor WI)*

'Eva went to work as a live-in maid at a farm when she left school. She remembers the coarse apron over the large white apron for mornings, with a cap, then a change in the afternoon into a small apron with frilly cap. Once one of the daughters of the house asked her mother, "Why does Eva have to wear those clothes, Mummy?" The answer came, "So that anyone who calls knows that she is the maid."

After that she went to work for a vicar. She had to learn to cook full meals for dinner parties, and read up a Mrs Beeton the vicar's wife lent her, in her spare time. She did well, and they were pleased with her, though she remembers being told that if the sons walked through the kitchen she was not to speak to them. She also had to call the vicar and his wife "Sir" and "Madam" at all times.' *(Londesborough WI)*

▧ Juvenile Service ▧

'It was always made very clear when we were children that everyone had to work for a living in the 1930s and 1940s. Books were considered to be time wasters in our house. We did

George Mackley, corn and flour dealer, Ellerker 1910. (John Harrison –
Bainton)

messages for neighbours, fetched the milk from the farm and
helped in the houses.

My brother's task was fetching the drinking water from the
village pump. At the age of twelve I had to work every Saturday
morning. By nine o'clock I was at the farmhouse where my father
worked. The house was very basic with no modern facilities, a
black leaded kitchen range with a side boiler the only means of
hot water. My first task was to wash, dry and clear away the
previous day's dishes and baking pots. The equipment was a
large enamel bowl and tin tray with a dish cloth. No washing up
liquid! I had to stand in a cold scullery. This took me about one
hour.

My second job was to scrub two kitchen tables, clear and scrub
the bottom pantry shelf, and when dry, replace all the items.
Another bucket of clean water and soap to scrub the red brick

Nanny (Nurse Betty) and Nanny's Help (Violet Soanes) on Bridlington beach with their young charges in 1929. (Shirley Franklin – Driffield WI)

kitchen floor, pantry and passage. This I hated doing as all the wellingtons and boots had thick dried mud on which immediately dropped off when moved.

The scullery floor was a mixture of red brick and stone, which had to be scrubbed, also the steps. After cleaning the buckets, I had finished, and it was twelve o'clock.

My take home pay was a shilling, which I had to take to the school Yorkshire Penny Bank. Sheer misery!' *(Marie Grice – Bainton WI)*

▨ The Village Wheelwright ▨

'Grandad was the village joiner, wheelwright and undertaker. I remember the red brick detached house in the yard down a quiet lane in the 1930s. The yard was a hotch potch of items, with a large hand cart which he used to transport the items he made, such as gates, tumbrels, stools, washing tubs, baking boards and coffins. Sometimes carts and waggons would be there for repairs. Piles of wood rested on the fence, and in a corner was a large hand-driven grindstone where the foresters came to sharpen their axes and knives.

I remember the workshop with the door always open, paint of every colour daubed on the inside from Grandad cleaning the paint brushes. The workshop had a smell of its own, a mixture of putty, pitch, sawdust, linseed oil and glue. There was a row of boxes with screws and nails of different sizes, and on the bench were many tools and the vice. How I loved watching him using the brace and bit and the planes. I remember the picture frames hanging up, the brass dial of the weight with the long chains and pan where he weighed the nails. Used glass stacked in an untidy pile. In the centre stood the well worn trestles, maybe a coffin in the making. This is where I was invited to help by holding the flock lining while he tacked it into position and then the braid gave a well finished look. Once Grandad asked me to make a small pillow with the flock; this was stuffed with wood shavings and sealed. Sometimes he gave me 2/- for doing this. *(Marie Grice – Bainton WI)*

WAR&PEACE

The Great War 1914-1918

There are still those who recall the upheaval and tragedy of the First World War, when civilians on the East Coast faced bombardment for the first time and every family experienced the pain of separation and loss.

▣ The First Aeroplane ▣

'When the Great War started in 1914 I was eight years old. We lived near to the police house in Nightingale Row at Rudston. We had heard about the Zeppelins that came over the East Coast on moonlit nights. Sometimes they dropped explosives, particularly at Scarborough where the German gunboats entered the bay and bombarded the town. We knew that aeroplanes were used along the coastline but we had not seen them in our village.

One morning an aeroplane flew low over Rudston. It circled, then made an emergency landing in a field of clover at Woldgate Top. It had a damaged wing and the canvas covering was torn so it was not safe to fly. The pilot was the son of a local family, Mr and Mrs Stevenson of Spring Dale, and he had wanted to see his home and village from the air.

Word spread very quickly that a plane had landed and for most people it was the first chance to see one. During that day everyone from Rudston and Burton Agnes, as well as the farms around, made their way to the corner field where the two lanes met. My mother put my little sister Ivy in her pram and we walked two miles to see something that we had never seen before!

Young Stevenson had found help and the wing was repaired. No other work was done that day as it was an exciting time for everyone. When the pilot climbed into the cockpit, ready to take off, three local men stood at each side of the plane holding the wing tips. As the plane moved across the grass they ran behind lifting the wings as it left the ground, cheered on by the crowd.

Members of the Waggoners Reserve of the First World War, formed by Sir Mark Sykes, at Sancton Grange. (John Harrison – Bainton)

The Waggoners Monument at Sledmere, erected after the First World War. (Isobel Shepherdson – Stamford Bridge WI)

Now it was time to go home. The excitement was over but not forgotten. For the next few weeks every detail was exchanged in conversation. It was the highlight of the year.' *(Hilda Pickering – Driffield WI)*

▣ CHURCH COMFORTS ▣

'This anecdote was told to me by my grandmother. Born in 1864 she had many of the Victorian standards, including the ban on all "work" on Sunday. This, of course, included any knitting, sewing etc.

However, when the First World War started, the vicar of the church attended by my grandmother told the women in his congregation that those who were knitting socks for the men in the Forces should bring their work to the service and should continue to knit during the sermon.

She felt it was a pleasant thought, that the "comforts" for the troops were produced during the church service at home.' *(Mollie Hunter – Patrington WI)*

▣ POWS AND PEACE ▣

'Mr Hunter was born during the war and spoke of the time when, as a toddler, he woke up frightened and crying every morning. The family lived in a cottage on the main street in Hook and every morning, very early, he could hear the heavy tramp of marching feet. This turned out to be the German POWs being escorted through the village and down to the river bank, where they were put to work reinforcing the earthen banks. They were billeted in the old schoolroom.

He was four years old in 1919, when all the children were given a Peace medal. He can't remember what was on it but it was made of tin. There was a parade round the village and everyone took part. All were in fancy dress of some sort, adults and children. He particularly remembers a boy called Cliff Moss who had only one leg, through TB, and was dressed as a wounded soldier.

There was also a man called Jammy Watson dressed up as a "black and white man". His costume was divided vertically, half black and half white. This became the trademark of the family. For years afterwards, at all village events, there was always a Watson as a "black and white man".

The Peace parade ended in Chapel Acres where a big bonfire was lit. There were fireworks and they all sang and cheered when they threw "Old Kaiser Bill" on the fire.' (*Edgar Hunter, of Hook*)

Yorkshire Dragoons at the blacksmith's forge. (Isobel Shepherdson – Stamford Bridge WI)

LIFE DURING THE SECOND WORLD WAR
1939 -1945

When war came again just 20 years later, everyone was involved. We coped with air raids, rationing, loss and destruction, and still somehow managed to carry on as normally as possible. Many local people have terrible memories of the bombing raids in both village and city, and of the days when even those working the land could be machine-gunned in the fields.

▣ WHEN WAR BROKE OUT ▣

'I was born in Hull in the early 1930s and was part of a small community, going to the local school with all my friends, and having aunts, uncles and cousins living nearby.

Our annual holidays were always taken at one of the East Coast resorts, usually Withernsea or Hornsea. It was on one of these that I first became aware of much anxiety around me. Children in those days were often excluded from adult conversations, all that I could gather was that something awful was about to take place. People were putting sand into bags on the beach, and there was talk of us coming home early, which in fact we did. Everyone spoke quietly about war, but this was before television, so that I had no idea what it all meant.

Eventually we heard on the radio that war had been declared, and our life changed. Soon we were standing in long lines waiting to be given our gas masks, from then on we carried them everywhere we went.

The next big event was the talk of closing the school, and everyone being evacuated. Our school was to go to Scarborough. Along with the teachers, some mothers were to go along and help, my mother being one of these. The thrill of going to this big house (a boarding house) and deciding who would sleep where!

Although we were constantly getting lost on the wrong landing, we all settled in fairly well. I was one of the lucky ones as I had my mother and sister all in the same room.

We shared a school with the local children, some going in the morning, some in the afternoon. On sunny days we all trooped down to the beach with our books and our teachers and had our lessons there, although playing in the sand was all we really wanted to do.

All this came to a sudden end when my sister became very ill with diphtheria and was rushed off to the local fever hospital. After her eventual recovery we went back to Hull, as all she wanted was to go home and see her Dad.

My father spent the war years in the Auxiliary Fire Service, and was for a long time stationed on Victoria Dock in Hull. Although he would never talk about his experiences, I later heard of the dangers and difficulties he and his colleagues faced during the awful air raids.

When we arrived home our school was closed and our friends were still away, but they came back gradually, and one day we saw a notice go up outside the school telling us it would reopen the following Monday.

The air raids started in Hull in 1941, and from then on we spent many nights in the communal air raid shelters in the school playground. We would run down the street as soon as the siren sounded, the air raid wardens urging us on and blowing their whistles. All this was in total darkness because of the black-out, although sometimes there were searchlights overhead. We could hear the German planes and ran very quickly to the shelters. Before long everyone had their "own place", ours being two bunks near the middle, my sister and I sharing one, my mother sitting on the one below. During heavy raids you could hear the bombs whistling down and when they exploded the whole shelter shook. The wardens were always on hand to help and keep everyone informed. The first question was always, "Has our street been hit?"

Because of the frequency of the raids we went to bed half-dressed and all the family slept in the front room, so we were ready to go into the shelter immediately we heard the sirens. During the early spring of 1941 there were many such occasions. My sister and I would be urged on by our mother to run, but she was always lagging behind, and it wasn't until a few years later that I connected the arrival of a brother in June of that year with her inability to run!

The number of local alerts for the whole of the war years was 815 (82 when high explosive and incendiary bombs were dropped). Our street was hit quite a few times and neighbours were killed, and our house had all the windows and doors blown out when an incendiary bomb dropped on the house opposite. We spent a few weeks at my grandparents' house on the outskirts of the city while repairs were carried out.

At one point during the war the authorities decided it was too dangerous to stay in the city at night, and arranged lorries to pick people up during the evening. We were then transported to villages a few miles away to sleep in village halls. As children we thought this great fun and sang heartily all the way. This arrangement didn't last long and soon we were back to the old routine of broken nights. Our school life was frequently disrupted depending on how many hours the air raids lasted.

Our very welcome summer holiday was a week at an aunt's house in a village near Tadcaster, Yorkshire. We talked about it for weeks, and couldn't wait for the day to come. We travelled on the bus from Hull to York and then on to Tadcaster, what a long journey it seemed to us. I enjoyed the travelling but my sister suffered travel-sickness and it was a great embarrassment to me sharing a seat with her. My aunt would be waiting at the bus-stop for us and with much excitement we arrived at her cottage.

What joy it was to get completely undressed and into our night-gowns and sleep undisturbed. I remember having to be reminded and reassured that I was safe, although even then I was half listening for aircraft. We walked in the countryside and most exciting of all, paddled in the nearby river, often having picnics there. I can never remember it raining, although I'm sure it must have done.

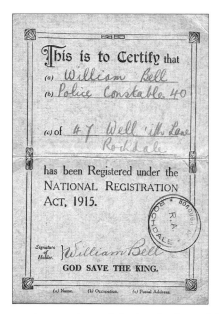

Identity cards were issued during both world wars.
(Olive Middlewood – Kilham WI)

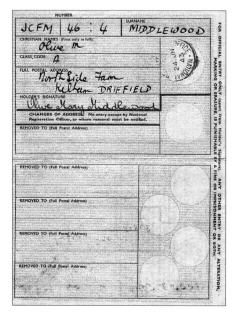

Back in Hull life resumed the daily routines, and as the war progressed the raids were less frequent. As everywhere else, we all knew of people being killed and occasionally saw the dreaded "telegram boys" knocking on neighbours' doors with sad news.

What a wonderful day it was when the war was finally over, and how we celebrated. Street parties were hastily organised and food produced from somewhere. The whole street was festooned with flags and bunting, and along with the rest of the country we had a lovely time. As we all had shared the difficult war years, so together we shared the Victory celebrations.' *(Freda Hobson – Rawcliffe WI)*

▩ ON THE ESTATE ▩

'My husband Frank was born at Easthorpe Farm, belonging to the Londesborough Estate. He went to school in the village, which meant a good walk over Chapel Hill, then down towards The Cascade, crossing the stream by the locally named Postman's Bridge. They kept two goats at Easthorpe, Blanche and Blossom, and Frank, at the age of ten, had the job of milking them each morning. It was wartime, 1940/41 and the army had moved into Londesborough. They installed a searchlight on Chapel Hill with soldiers on regular guard duty. When Frank set off for school each day he could be seen carrying, along with his school satchel, a can of milk. On Chapel Hill he would stop with his special delivery – goats' milk for the soldiers, which he sold to them at sixpence a pint.

Children from the village and surrounding farms did quite well from the soldiers stationed at Londesborough, who provided a variety of fun and games. Frank remembers them giving a party especially for the neighbouring children, who were collected from the surrounding farms and cottages in an army lorry. It was an unforgettable treat, causing a great bustle of excitement.

The Booths were the owners of Londesborough Estate at that time and Mrs Booth's Christmas parties for the village children were very special occasions. One treat she particularly liked to give was to scatter handfuls of toffees over the fence into the school yard. The children, in their turn, delighted in the mad scramble for the prize of a tasty sweet or two. The youngsters got up to lots of antics. Encouraged by the soldiers they made bows and arrows from the bamboo that grew in front of Londesborough Park. The army, mainly officers, were billeted there for most of the wartime period.

This was, of course, well before I met and married Frank. I lived at South Farm in Thorpe-le-Street, which was hardly a hamlet, never mind a village. It is situated midway between Shiptonthorpe and Hayton, and was part of the Everingham Estate belonging to the Duke of Norfolk. It comprised two farmhouses and two cottages. It was lovely there when I was a girl.

My father did mixed farming, livestock and arable. During the war we considered ourselves well away from the besieged cities. One night, however, a bomb dropped in the front paddock adjoining our house. The roof was badly damaged. Nearly all the tiles were blown off in the blast, and two ceilings came down. Many sheep, and two horses, were killed – a cart-horse and a hunter. A pony, Betty, was injured with shrapnel and many weeks afterwards she had to be destroyed, the vets having done all they could.

"Why us?" everyone said. Was it that the German planes thought we were a search-light point? Or was it that they were emptying left-over bombs before returning to base? The event caused much speculation and concern. The bomb fell with an almighty thud and people said it was a good job it hadn't hit the road. The blast was seen from afar. The first to arrive on the scene was a Mr Thorpe. "It's miraculous! It's miraculous!" my two sisters and I heard him exclaim. How brave he was to come on his bicycle alone from Shiptonthorpe, not knowing what he was going to find around 9 pm in early March.

We didn't have shelters in the country. There was a siren at Market Weighton police station, and if it went, and it was a dreadful noise when it did, Mother put us all in the passageway that went between the dairy, the side door and the breakfast room. She thought it the safest place in the house and made it comfortable, with mattresses and blankets on the floor. A Royal Air Force couple were billeted in North Farm farmhouse across the road. They were kindly people and after the blast they gave up a double bed for us girls. It was a squash, three to a bed, but we didn't mind, we were just glad to be unharmed and together. Friends in Wilberfoss had us for the next day. Our mother still managed to provide a seventh birthday tea for my youngest sister two days after the event. People were very good.

At Melbourne, in the Derwent valley, there was a prisoner of war camp. Some of the Italian prisoners came to work on the farm. They were very nice people. They made me a ring from a thru'penny-bit. When they'd finished carving out the centre to make the shiny octagonal circlet for my finger, they carved my name on the inner rim. I still have it.' *(Dorothy Stevenson, via Audrey Dunne – Londesborough WI)*

'During the war the government requisitioned Londesborough Park for the allied forces, and Warrendale Farm was used as a wireless station. The army also commandeered the village concert hall and several other farms and houses. Everyone, whether they liked it or not, was pulled into what was called "The War Effort". The main personnel in Londesborough were Signals and the Military Police. The stables were taken over by the Army Motor Transport Depot. Soldiers of the Third Hussars were billeted elsewhere and everywhere in the village, some of them the remnants from Dunkirk. A searchlight was installed on the higher ground of Londesborough Park, but there were no guns.

Allied planes could often be seen on practice manoeuvres circling high above the Wolds. One day a fighter plane and a Halifax bomber accidentally collided. Although the fighter lost a wing, the pilot and crew managed to bail out to safety. The Halifax, however, though it seemed to be going well at first, turned over, spiralling into a crash on the edge of Saxon Wood, on the northerly part of the estate towards Park Farm. It had been carrying a number of young Frenchmen. They were all killed. It was a terrible and sudden confrontation with the reality of war, and all for nothing too. An awful waste of young life.' *(Sonny Harrison, via Audrey Dunne – Londesborough WI)*

▣ WAR AT FANGFOSS ▣

'During the war, we had total blackout, noises of guns and aircraft – and gas masks. In cardboard boxes, they were carried everywhere with string slung over our shoulders. They often held our milk money, war savings money, and even our precious few pocket money pennies sometimes. The gas masks smelled of dust and rubber and were stifling to wear. Gas drill was not a fun time.

The Vale of York was criss-crossed by airfields, which meant close contact with Polish, Canadian, Norwegian and other allied airmen as well as our own men. Memories are still vivid of planes that crash-landed, the horrible deaths by fire of some crewmen, of enemy aircraft droning around in search of targets, of the shock of falling bombs dropping out of "the blue".

In 1939 there had been the first rush of evacuees from Sunderland and Hull. Some of the children had never seen the country before and felt very strange. Everyone's life was turned upside down. The village children suddenly acquired new "brothers and sisters" with strange ways. School classes were taken in school, the village hall, the parish hall, and the Methodist schoolroom.

By 1940 there were soldiers on manoeuvres in the area, and later in the war a prisoner of war camp was built outside Fangfoss to house Italian POWs. These men made lovely wooden toys – acrobats tumbling up and down a stick, pecking hens etc, and wooden boxes. One much prized pokerwork box is still in use today. Some prisoners came out to work on the land and often had their hunks of fat bacon supplemented by a slice of apple pie or whatever was going.

Throughout the war there were endless fundraising events. One year a concert for Wings For Victory, given by Bishop Wilton WI, was held in Fangfoss school. And there was always the tea

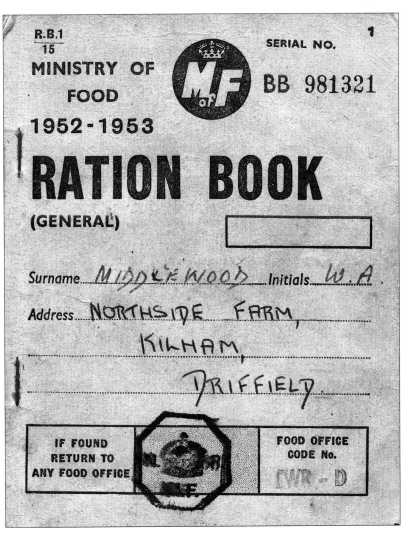

R.B.1
15

MINISTRY OF
FOOD
1952-1953

SERIAL NO.

BB 981321

RATION BOOK

(GENERAL)

Surname MIDDLEWOOD Initials W.A.

Address NORTHSIDE FARM,
KILHAM,
DRIFFIELD.

IF FOUND
RETURN TO
ANY FOOD OFFICE

FOOD OFFICE
CODE No.

FWR - D

Rationing began very soon after the war started — and continued for several years after it ended! (Olive Middlewood – Kilham WI)

to be ladled out to troops on manoeuvres, and tea and sandwiches when meeting the trains of children on trips.

Women were conscripted during the war. There were some reserved occupations, but all able-bodied women who hadn't already volunteered for some sort of service had to fill in a long form if they needed to apply for exemption to call-up. I remember an apocryphal story of the weary farmer's wife who filled in the details of her weekly round of feeding the hens; collecting, cleaning and packing the eggs; feeding the livestock; milking; butter and cheese making; washing; cooking; baking; supplying all the farm workers and family with breakfast, drinkings, dinner, and tea and generally caring for the needs of a household of twelve; and that was apart from haymaking, the harvest, potatoing etc, etc. And then she came to the space that asked, "What do you do in your spare time?" After much thought she wrote, "I go to the toilet".' *(Ella Musgrove for Fangfoss with Bolton WI)*

▣ HULL UNDER FIRE ▣

'When the war commenced the Naval Base came to the road where I was living. A few houses were requisitioned and the families had to move out. In those days most houses were rented.

As my mother owned her home and had four teenage children living there, she was given permission to stay, on condition that she had Captain Chichester to live there. He was related to the Chichester-Constables of Burton Constable. He was in charge of the base and the other ranks were billeted in houses nearby.

I was in Shipping and was reserved. Among my jobs I was decoding for the convoys. We looked after the captains while they were in port and they used to bring stockings home for us.

I had to learn First Aid and how to use a stirrup pump for the incendiary bombs which were dropped first in the raids. My young sister and I had to fire watch each night after work as soon as the sirens were blown. We were accompanied by Mr Hunt the optician and Mr Rapstone the antiques dealer. We all had to walk up and down the road, passing the sailors on sentry duty and having a laugh and a chat. When the 'all clear' went, my mother had a drink ready for us. This went on night after night and then in the morning we wondered who had been unlucky. We soon found out when we read of the many deaths in the paper.

I was due to get married and was lucky to get some lovely lace material for my dress. Much to the amusement of everyone packed in the shelter, it was the first thing I took when there was an air raid.

However bad the damage was, everyone worked hard to find spare rooms to keep going. One day I arrived at the office to find one of my young clerks wasn't in the office. His father was the Dock Master and he used to laugh and say "only a land mine" would do damage, and it did – the family were killed.' *(Diana Best – Cottingham WI)*

▨ RAINING DOWN ON HULL ▨

'In early May of 1941, the bombs were raining down on Hull almost nightly. I lived in the "Avenues" with my parents and had been moved from school to school as each became damaged or destroyed. We sheltered each night in the passage between our house and the one next door, which had sand bags at either end. My father was a fire watcher and spent nights watching for incendiary bombs and coping with small fires and damage. My mother always wore a whistle on a piece of string round her neck, "in case we get hit, and the rescuers would be able to find us in the rubble", she said.

In summers previously she took a cottage at Hornsea or Withernsea for two weeks, for a holiday. This year both places were full of evacuees so she made enquiries elsewhere with the same result. However, a friend of our family told her of a caravan on the cliff top at Aldbrough which was available for two weeks. She took it.

My three sisters were doing war work; the oldest one, a war widow with a little girl, we took with us. When we arrived – what an adventure! It was a converted charabanc, with bunk beds that folded up into table and seats. It had a stove that my mother cooked on, shelves high up with pots and pans and crisp frilly curtains at every window. More exciting to us children were soldiers on guard every few yards, some in little trenches in the cliffs. Beyond was the blue open sea. We were not allowed to go down to the beach but we were always watching something happening everyday. We heard bits of conversations that didn't mean anything to us at the time, words like "invasion", "challenge" and "halt". We children thought it was a wonderful new game.

Towards the end of the second week a lady we made friends with next door asked my mum if she would like to buy a bungalow as it had come up for sale. The owner's wife had died in a raid, with her children in Hull, and he was a ship's captain who would be away for a long time. The asking price was £60 fully furnished. It was made of wood, and had two large bedrooms, a living room and kitchen and a long verandah the whole length of the front. The furniture included real brass bedsteads, ornate dressing tables with swing mirrors, and a gold plush seven piece suite, two large carved arm chairs, four dining chairs and a chaise longue, all to match. Also a huge carved sideboard with high back and large mirrors and shelves, real mahogany. After much thought my mother bought it!

We three moved in, and my father and sisters visited us when they could. Most nights, at dusk we would watch airplanes pass over going to Hull, and many long fingers of searchlights sweeping the sky. In due time, my niece and I started the village school. My first surprise there was that the cloakroom was stacked high with parcels, sacks and boxes – invasion rations, we found out later.' *(Faith Wilson – Holme on Spalding Moor WI)*

⬛ DANTE AND BEANO ⬛

'I grew up in a small village outside Scarborough where my father owned a small shop to sell butter and eggs and other products. Because of this, he owned a lorry with a cover over the top in which he used to take produce to Scarborough market every week. There were very few vehicles around at that time and he would often do people's shopping for them in Scarborough and bring it home.

In the summer time, my mother, aunties and cousins would all pack into the lorry along with half the village and go to Primrose

Valley for a picnic. We took along an upright tent in which to change and we spent the day on the beach. My father went back to the shop and returned in the evening to pick us all up. We felt very privileged and we took as many people as would fit in the truck.

During the war, the same truck had to be registered as an ambulance in order to get a petrol allowance. If there was an invasion, then the truck had to go to Humnanby, where it was given a code word. Our truck's code word was "Dante". After the war the horse *Dante* ran in the Derby and because of the connection, my Dad put a bet on it. It was the first and only time my father ever betted. And, of course, it won!

Frank was an air raid warden during the war and he suffered with asthma. If ever there was a raid, Frank would get the warning by phone. He would then get on his bike and blow his whistle on the road to Folkton. We had a dog called Beano who would hear the warning from Bridlington long before Frank got his phone call. He would bark and my father would be out helping Frank, long before he knew officially.' *(Maisie Lilley – Bempton WI)*

▣ MACHINE-GUNNED IN THE FIELDS ▣

'It was shortly after the war started, in the summer of 1940, when one night after school my sister and I went to watch my father haymaking in the field. He was sitting on the hayrake, being drawn by a white horse.

Suddenly, without any warning, a German plane dived down out of the sky and started machine-gunning us. Father shouted to us to run to the edge of the field and lay down in the ditch. We were terrified but we ran as fast as our legs could carry us and laid in the bottom of the ditch. Father had taken his horse near to a big hedge for shelter and he lay down on the ground.

The German plane flew menacingly round and started machine-gunning again, but fortunately it eventually flew away and we all went safely home. It was a very frightening experience and I still remember it very clearly.' *(Mrs G. Beadle – Burstwick WI)*

◨ CORSETS ON TOP ◨

'One night during the early part of the war, my boyfriend and I had just arrived home after an evening at the pictures when the sirens went. My mother and father were upstairs in bed asleep. Some minutes later my mother came rushing down the stairs in a panic, on her way to the air raid shelter. She was fully clothed with her lace-up corsets on top!' *(Mrs Beesley – Cottingham Green WI)*

◨ NAFFERTON HALL ◨

'My grandfather owned Nafferton Hall, a 200 year old house, which initially to my memory was gas-lit and had electricity laid on only around 1935. Beautiful, clean, potable water was drawn by hand-pump near the wash-house and cooking was done on a huge black-leaded, coal or wood fired kitchen range. Washing was done manually with zinc tubs, posters and hand mangles. The hall was reputedly haunted, and observed by Grandma and Grandpa.

The milkman cycled daily down the drive and round the village with churns balanced on the handlebars. Butter, meat and cheese were freely available from the local farming community and in fact butter was made with a hand-churn at the Hall. We had roaring, open log fires for heating (no central heating), a billiard room and a tennis court on the front lawn.

The war in 1939 brought a markedly different situation, because as the house had 13 acres of ground, some fields were commandeered by the military for Nissen huts in which soldiers were billeted. From 1940 to 1942 a succession of prisoners of war were housed in camps in Nafferton, initially Italians in a specially built camp on the outskirts of the village.

These POWs were "trusties", employed on farm work, and wandered freely in the area, never escaping. The Italians were very excitable, but likeable and traded trinkets, like rings or "jewelry" they had made in camp, for some food, but more often for soap.

Eventually they were transported elsewhere and German

POWs were placed on Grandad's land. They were also "trusties" and very nice lads to get on with. I was learning German at school and they helped me with spoken language quite a lot.

The attitude towards these Germans was very free and easy in the village and, together with their guards, they frequently came to the Hall for a drink of beer and a game of billiards. They also helped in the garden and with heavier household tasks, like chopping wood and digging.

When they moved elsewhere, French Algerian troops were in Nafferton. These were all very tall (6ft 6in and over) and ebony black. Again, they were fine fellows to get on with, and I could practice my schoolboy French with them. We made good friends with many of these Free French Algerians, who eventually were involved with the invasion landings in Algeria, when many were killed, unfortunately.

Of course, during all of this period, heavy bombing raids were taking place on Hull (particularly), Sheffield, Manchester and Liverpool by the Luftwaffe. I mention this because in Nafferton we became very blase about this almost nightly occurrence. The house shook and rattled violently from nearby anti-aircraft guns and from stray bombs, mines etc aimed at Hull.

Nafferton Hall and grounds had a large patch of woodland around it and it was said to be a very characteristic landmark from the air. Consequently, before setting off to bomb Germany, RAF bombers from Driffield, Langtoft, Cranswick, Leconfield etc rendezvoused over Nafferton, before heading for the Continent. We always knew when something was "on", because groups of 20 to 30 aircraft would circle overhead, then depart, to be replaced by more about 30 minutes later.

Ironically, the German aircraft also used the Nafferton "landmark", and we frequently observed Dorniers and Heinkels caught in searchlight beams over the Hall. On one occasion we were disturbed by V1 doodlebugs, on their way to the West Riding.

All throughout war time, we visited Bridlington in summer, bathed, made sand castles and played on the beach without restriction. Occasionally, a German aircraft passed over the coast in daylight, but nobody took any notice.

Shortly after 1946, my grandparents died and Nafferton Hall was sold.' *(Eric Longbottom, of Cottingham)*

⊠ On an Egg! ⊠

'At the end of May 1944 my uncle had been working in the fields and arrived home tired and weary around eight o'clock in the evening, at his farm in Rawcliffe.

Waiting at the front of his farmstead were two officers of the Royal Engineers. They civilly greeted Uncle Billy and proceeded to inform him they were to commandeer parts of his farm buildings for 360 soldiers. He had quite a lot of empty stables that he had used for hunters.

The troops moved in, swept down cobwebs, hosed floors and set up a cook house. A railway carriage that was used by the tennis club was to be the four officers' accommodation. The soldiers lived there for a week, with delicious smells drifting from the cook house. The officers' residence was guarded 24 hours a day by sentries with fixed bayonets.

On the Saturday evening one of the officers tapped on Uncle

Members of the Woodmansey Home Guard c1944.
(J. Wilson – Kilham WI)

Billy's door. "Is it possible for you to exchange 360 eggs for a carton of corned beef, so I can give my men a treat?" The eggs were duly delivered to the cook house.

The Sunday was spent clearing and packing up and Monday morning the troops had all gone, not leaving a trace of evidence behind, except a notice on one of the walls saying "Careless talk costs lives!"

Uncle Billy, Auntie Edie and Barbara were eating their lunch on Wednesday and had the radio on. There was a news flash – "The Allied Forces have landed in France!" Uncle Billy looked at Auntie Edie and Barbara and solemnly said, "On an egg!" It was 6th June 1944.' *(Brenda Kelly – Marshland WI)*

▣ MEMORIES OF RUDSTON ▣

'A member has memories of seeing her mother who kept a shop patiently threading food coupons (points) on to a thread so they were all fastened together each week.

A member who worked in Whiteleys shop on the Promenade in Bridlington, a ladies' outfitters, haberdashery and household furnishings, curtaining etc, remembers the queues outside the shop on the day rationing ended and their having a complete sell out of curtain material.

Memories of having brown paper tape criss-crossed over the school windows to prevent glass shattering in the event of bomb damage and of having to have blackout curtains and blinds for all windows to obliterate all light. We had to go to the village hall in Sledmere for worship because the church couldn't be used as it wasn't possible for the windows to be blacked out properly.

My husband remembers having "gas mask practice" at school when everyone had to don the gas masks that had to be carried everywhere. Presumably this was to become accustomed to putting them on and to become used to wearing them. I imagine it must have been quite a sight to see 30 or more children snuffing and snorting inside those things. I don't think anyone who ever wore one of them will ever forget its very distinctive smell!

He also recalls having to have his gas mask replaced very

frequently because he and his brother used to walk quite a distance to school each day over the fields, bouncing it on the ground at every step. They passed an army camp en route and the soldiers awaiting their passing each day greeted them with jam sandwiches, which would no doubt help them on their walk home. I suppose some of these soldiers would have children of their own at home and would be pleased to see them enjoying a treat. The soldiers were always eager to 'barter' some of their jam supplies in exchange for fresh eggs from the farm on which they lived.

A member recalls that in the event of an air raid occurring whilst they were at school – which did happen since they were quite close to Driffield airfield – the village children were allowed to go home whilst those who lived outside the village were sent to various houses in the village. She questions the wisdom of the procedure of standing in the churchyard being told to disperse to their various destinations and also recalls some of the boys who didn't return to school!

The same member reports that her husband's two sisters joined the Land Army and were posted to Wiltshire. Whilst working in the potato fields one day, there were some soldiers on manoeuvres and who should come crawling through their field on hands and knees but a young man from their own village of Rudston.

A member who lived at Sledmere in close proximity to a searchlight battery, remembers her father digging out a large hole, lining it with wood, covering over the top with corrugated metal sheets, then covering over the lot with stones and soil, thereby creating an air raid shelter for the family. Each member of the family had responsibility for another, her task being to see Grandma safely to the shelter. She recalls that Grandma insisted on wearing her hat to go down and on one such occasion she got her safely into the shelter, whereupon Grandma removed the hat and promptly put it down over the candle, thereby plunging them all into darkness.

Sledmere school was bursting at the seams accommodating an influx of evacuees from the South Shields and Newcastle-upon-Tyne areas, whilst a member who attended Hutton Cranswick school says their evacuees were from the Hull area. In all cases there were some children who didn't return home afterwards.

Several members can remember prisoners of war camps locally, with barbed wire around them and guard towers at the corners. The prisoners were talented in making things from odds and ends they found lying around, like a ring made from bone, slippers made from plaited binder twine and beautiful toys made from scraps of wood. Several recalled the "pecking hens" made from something resembling a table tennis bat, with a weight suspended beneath causing the hens to "peck" in succession. The details burnt on to the wood were remarkable. These would be made in the evenings since many of the prisoners worked on farms during the day.' *(Barbara Moorcroft – Rudston WI)*

▣ THE CANCELLED MATINEE ▣

'Bank Holiday Monday, 1942 was a slightly cloudy day. Nothing had created much excitement in Goole in the previous months, though we had witnessed the tragedies of our gallant bomber crews crashing in and around the area on several occasions – Goole was ringed by a number of bomber airfields. Many evenings we could see the red flares and glow in the sky in the direction of Hull.

My brother and I had gone out for a walk in the town. At about one o'clock there suddenly appeared an aircraft out of the low cloud. We were walking along the pavement when suddenly I saw the nose-gunner swinging his machine gun, and bullets were peppering the pavement beside us. Terrified, we ran to a shop doorway, where the proprietor and his wife hastily dragged us inside and we all went under his counter.

We heard bombs falling from the aircraft. We learned later that there had been some considerable casualties, two of them fatal, and much damage. The bombs had landed in a built-up area, close to a popular picture house. The matinee had been cancelled that day. If that had not been so, there would have been many children and young adults converging on the cinema and a large queue snaking round the corner into the street where the bombs fell. The thought of what might have happened fills one with horror. The cancellation must have been "by the grace of God".

My future husband was staying with his grandparents near Pocklington at the time and nearby was an army gun crew. They shot down the Luftwaffe bomber and it ended its days in the River Humber. He watched all the action.' *(Brenda Kelly – Marshland WI)*

LIFE AS A LAND GIRL

Many girls decided to enlist as land girls in the Women's Land Army, preferring an outdoor life to that in the munitions factory or the Services. It was not always as romantic as the posters of the time promised!

▨ A LAND GIRL'S DILEMMA ▨

'I was a city girl through and through. I worked as an apprentice hairdresser in a salon on Hessle Road, in Hull. Hairdressing was not an essential occupation in wartime England. It was classed as a "luxury job". The two women who owned the business were called up and the shop was closed. I was seventeen-and-a-half and didn't know what I would do for work. A friend, who knew of my dilemma, suggested we offer ourselves for government work as land girls. I was always ready for an adventure and agreed to do it. If I could get into the nearby hostel for land girls in Hessle, I would be able to earn a bit of extra money by doing hairdressing in the evenings. However, there were no vacancies in the hostel. I was accepted for the work, but was directed to a private farm at Rillington, in the Derwent valley, miles away from Hull.

Land girls on an East Riding farm. (John Harrison – Bainton)

Mr Exley, the farmowner, met us, an inexperienced litter of land girls, in his car at Malton railway station. For us "townies" it was a scary journey to Low Farm, meandering along narrow lanes and through gated fields. We huddled together in the back of the car, searching one another with unanswerable questions: "Wherever are we? Where are we going? What am I doing here?"

As far as we were concerned we could just as easily have been on the moon. When we got to the farm Mr Exley, who was probably as nervous of us as we were of him, suggested, in straightforward country style, that, "Thee'd best get into thee working clo'as."

The land girl uniform was quite smart and I liked wearing it. It was all good quality clothing: strong corduroy trousers, a green jumper, airtex shirts, stout overalls, thick socks, gumboots, a wonderful heavy-duty coat and a land girl hat.

"We'll get yon cows up for milkin' first off," Mr Exley nodded in the direction of his herd of Ayrshires. Their massive horns waved about ferociously.

The idea was to get the cows into the stone stalls ready for milking. As he opened the door to the byre, the cows pressed in. I was quick to learn that it was necessary to keep one's head well out of the way of those horns. I was instructed to place chains around the cows' necks in order to hold them still for milking. They had machinery to do the actual milking, but I had to learn how to use it. One of the girls couldn't take to the cows at all. She quickly disappeared to help in the kitchen. Another girl only lasted a month. The work was hard, but I took to the country life and it wasn't long before I was broken into herding up the cows and getting them into the byre.

The pay was quite good for land girls – 30 shillings a week, plus food and board. We did our own washing on a massive wooden table in the kitchen, and there was a hand wringer to squeeze the water from the clothes. I was soon part of the family. I learned to drive the big lugwheel tractor, and then a car. One of the land girls carelessly drove the lugwheel tractor backwards over an expensive stack-sheet. It caused a lot of damage and she got into trouble for it. I took the Exleys' children to school in the car.

A land girl's wedding. (John Harrison – Bainton)

Sometimes I got the job of baby-sitting whilst the Exleys went to the pictures in Malton. One night, whilst they were out, a blustering gale arose. Suddenly a terrible moaning started up. It was coming from the byre and sounded like someone in dreadful pain. There was a big bull chained up out there and I wondered if he'd broken loose and injured somebody. I had to do something. Taking a storm lamp I ventured out into the bleak night. The lamp was almost blown out by the gale as I tussled across the yard.

When I got to the byre I found it wasn't the bull. A polled roan – a de-horned cow of mixed breeding – which had been put in a different stall from its usual one, had broken loose. Unhappy that another beast was in its place it was causing a rumpus. In the pandemonium the big-horned Ayrshire in the polled roan's stall had got its head twisted completely around. It was contorted in such a way as to prod itself in the rump with its own horns. Every movement it made tore at a gash in its side, causing the beast to let out a ghastly moan. I calmly, singlehandedly, and with some difficulty, tied up the butting, hornless roan, sorted out the wounded Ayrshire and, eventually, went back to the welcome warmth of the farmhouse.

Mr Exley had a Morris Eight. Each day 40 gallons of milk had to be taken into Malton on a trailer hooked to the back of the car. This was my job, and on the way into town I dropped the children off at school. Sometimes, as well as conveying the milk to the dairy, I also brought in a calf, destined for the cattle market in Yorkers' Gate. One day, on arriving at the dairy after handing over a calf, I was given a message. I had to report to the police station immediately.

"You're from Exleys'?" the duty officer inquired.

"Yes," came my reply.

"You've put a calf into market?"

"Yes, a bull-calf. I always do it."

"Well you're in trouble. There's foot and mouth disease. You're not allowed to move cattle about."

I protested I didn't know about the ban. Out at Low Farm the accumulator had run out. The wireless wouldn't work without an accumulator, and I hadn't had sight of a newspaper either. It took me a long time, but at last I convinced them I was innocent.

"Well, you'd best go and collect the calf, young woman," the police constable instructed. "And get a new accumulator while you're at it."

It was ridiculous, the things we did. I sometimes wonder how we ever got through. In the corner of the stack-yard was a clutter of scrapped motor vehicles. Mr Exley decided to rescue one of them for ferrying the children back and forth. It had no window-glass and was in an awful state. He got it going, but once it was going it mustn't be stopped as the starter-motor was done for. It happened that the weather was really bad, with lots of snow and ice. I was dutifully chugging along with the children in the back when we came upon a snow-plough clearing the road. I couldn't get past without manoeuvring a heap of packed snow on the far side. I daren't stop. The labourers on the snow-plough just stood back and stared as I steered the car up and over the mountain of ice and down the other side, slithering this way and that. I got the children to school alright – but had to be towed back.

And yet there was nothing quite like it; driving the tractor across the open field, the reaper and binder trundling behind, and above and beyond the great flocks of gulls wheeling and weaving in your wake. The Exleys were truly honest, decent farming folk, and I considered myself lucky to be with such a good family. We got on famously and remained lifelong friends.

Of course, cheeky young farmhands would sometimes have a laugh, making jokes about the "towny land girl".

"I can see you've got an 'airdresser for a land girl," they'd banter to Mr Exley, "by the curls and waves at bottom of yon field she's ploughed."

But it was well meant and I could take it, giving as good as I got. I think the truth was they really respected my ability to get on with the job. As for myself, I loved every minute of it.' *(Edna Cavill, via Audrey Dunne – Londesborough WI)*

Married Life

Getting married and setting up home had its own problems during the war, from the difficulty of organising the wedding to the prospect of long separation.

⬛ The Blitz Wedding ⬛

'My mother's older sister Annie was a happy lady who had given birth to 16 children, of which twelve survived. Her husband Frank pushed a handcart up and down Hessle Road in Hull, in the summer selling crabs and in the winter rabbits. I was the youngest of three sisters and loved to visit my Aunt Annie's house, in Staniforth Place.

It was 1941 and I was 17 years old. The youngest of my aunt's daughters was to be married to a soldier due home on leave. I was asked to be bridesmaid and as I was a trainee dressmaker, Aunt Annie said she would buy the material if I could make the dress. This when things were so scarce. Bemoaning this to a colleague in Hammonds workroom where I worked she offered me enough pretty floral georgette with lining for ten shillings. My wages at that time would be 15 shillings a week.

Making this dress was a trial, for when I started to sew in the evenings the air raid sirens would wail. My father was a club steward in Waltham Street in the centre of the town and Mother decided if we were to die in an air raid we would die together, so we would make a dash to join Father who had to stay at the club to firewatch. We usually just made it before the bombs started falling, my sister Doris a Red Cross nurse having rushed to the Hull Royal Infirmary to join the rest of the brave staff waiting to take care of the raid victims.

After one "all clear" we took our weary way home to Brunswick Road to find the house in turmoil, four air raid wardens searching through the place looking for a fire bomb which was seen going through the roof; it was found burnt out on a joist. The dress survived but only just – to enter the house the four wardens had climbed through a window and walked over it lying on a couch.

The wedding date was 8th May. Yes, the day after the blitz on Hull. That awful night Mother and I had no time to join Father before the bombs rained down. Crouched in a cupboard under the stairs that night of terror burns a hole in my memory which will live with me for ever, but we all survived. After a few hours' sleep a friend I worked with called to tell of the destruction of the city centre including our workplace, that wonderful store Hammonds with its beautiful oak staircase and an elegance which never returned.

The wedding had to go on as the bridegroom had only a few days' leave. I had a hair appointment at a shop called Meeks in Paragon Square. Surrounded by hosepipes, firemen, burnt out buildings, and wading through water I surprised the staff who thought I was mad expecting to have my hair done on such a horrific day, but when I explained why they pulled out all the

Getting married during the Hull blitz. (Edna Bradley – Hornsea WI)

stops and sent me on my way glamourised with only the aid of a small mug of water and a comb.

My next stop was my aunt's house to see if they had lived through the night. I found Allen the bridegroom standing on the doorstep looking forlorn. His objective was the same as mine but he had sent his sister indoors to ease his mind as his mother had told him he must not see Elsie the bride before the wedding as it was unlucky. In the circumstances I thought this hilarious!

The family all survived and the only loss was the flowers, the florist bombed into rubble. A search unearthed twelve tulips without a leaf or fern for me, which were very hard to control, and four roses for the bride.

I cannot remember much about the rest of the day as we all sailed through it in a daze of exhaustion and shock. The Germans came again that night so the honeymoon was spent in a shelter.

It is strange which memories of May 1941 stand out as a symbol of the devastation. Mine was seeing Mr Powell, a senior member of the family who founded Hammonds, then an old gentleman, walking through the ruins of his store, alone in his devastation.' *(Edna Bradley – Hornsea WI)*

⊠ No Cake? ⊠

'Preparing for our wedding we thought, "No cake!", but my Aunt Jane who made her own butter and cheese sent some butter wrapped in blankets (I still have the blankets) and Arthur's mother supplied the eggs, so we didn't have to use dried egg. My mother saved lots of dried fruit – a bit here, a bit there for weeks – and sugar, so we were more fortunate than many couples who did not have a cake at all. I think it was possible to get a few extra rations if you were having 40 guests, and my mother saved on other rations too, so we managed a sort of reception.

We bought some furniture in 1941 and I got curtaining. Again we were fortunate, as furniture went onto "dockets'" shortly afterwards and curtains were on coupons while we were on honeymoon. Lots of couples, of course, did not get a honeymoon. I have friends who spent theirs waiting two hours on York station for the husband's embarkation train. Another couple I know caught a train to London straight after their wedding, for him to get his train back to the front.

My dress was made by Elsie Battle (shops in Beverley and Bridlington). It was made of Chantilly lace, as lace was not on coupons. Flowers were a difficulty. We went to several florists but growers were concentrating on food, not flowers. However, a florist in Bridlington suggested sweetpeas and even managed posies of various flowers for the bridesmaids.

Gents' suits were 26 coupons, ladies' coats were, I think, the same. My mother managed a complete new outfit apart from new shoes. Hats were not on coupons. Wedding rings looked like curtain rings and were often not gold. I said I wouldn't have one, but the jeweller where my engagement ring was bought had just one 22 carat ring in stock, which he made smaller for me. Again, we were fortunate, and I'm still wearing it after nearly 55 years.' *(Olive Middlewood – Kilham WI)*

⊠ Getting By ⊠

'When war came I went to farming friends as a voluntary land girl. I tried ploughing with a pair of horses, forked manure, did

182

poultry work and made myself generally useful. I also fell in love with the farmer's son, and we were married in 1940 – a very quiet ceremony.

Being within a mile of the East Coast with only sand dunes between fields and sea, there was a restriction on travel, so few people could get a pass to join in the marriage service in the village church of Barmston. No fuss – a navy dress with red blouse effect under bolero. At least I can boast it was a 'Susan Small' model. I wore a borrowed navy "halo" hat in jersey material with diamante clips to brighten it up! Only the family joined us for a drink of port and piece of cake, made with rationed ingredients. Then we had a five day honeymoon in Grasmere, travelling by train. Bliss!

The army moved in on our farm – soldiers after Dunkirk who lived in tents and granaries. Officers were billeted in the farmhouse, two with smart young wives. I learned to cook and clean with my mother-in-law to teach me. The washing up was done on the kitchen table in a zinc bowl, and rationing made cooking very restricted, though we had extra rations for farm workers – eggs, and more bacon and ham when we were permitted to kill a pig!

We moved into a poor house, unbelievably primitive and badly neglected, as tenants in 1942. It was hard work, with no electricity, septic tank or luxuries.

I became pregnant, and knew nothing of such a condition. It was a "taboo" subject for unmarried girls, and my older sisters had told me nothing of childbirth. No mention in magazines either!

So, I continued with life, trying to ignore the prospect of the coming birth, but eventually braved a visit to our nice family doctor after four months! I was examined, and told to book in for January in the local maternity home, and just went on getting larger and more embarrassed. The travelling butcher even looked sideways at me before saying, "I don't want to be personal, but shouldn't you have applied for extra meat coupons!"

My mother helped with sewing and knitting and bought terry

towelling nappies. My sister lent smocks for my increasing girth, and I stitched elastic loops to my skirts.

I had seen many animals give birth, but still didn't recognise the symptoms of labour when I happened to be alone on the farm, other than workmen. My husband was selling a cow 50 miles away. We had no telephone, so a boy was dispatched on a bicycle. Still not sure about being in labour I was driven to the home and within an hour had a baby boy. What a shock! Once "delivered" I felt fine, and could have got up the next day – but no. "If you put your feet to the ground in less than ten days – everything could drop!"

So I had a fortnight's rest – feeding my baby and reading when not embroidering vyella night gowns for him. No need for other baby clothes other than jackets ("matinee") and shawls for the first six weeks. I had a baby-care book given by Mother, and followed the advice of four-hourly feeds etc, with baby fitting in with farmhouse routine!

Four babies in less than five years! I never bought a bottle, going straight from breast milk to boiled cow's milk in a cup. I had part time help, a good husband – but could have done without the two farm lads living in!' *(Irene Megginson – Bishop Wilton WI)*

▣ COMING HOME ▣

'It was November 1945. I was sitting in the cinema with my parents watching *Mrs Miniver* when to my amazement my name flashed up on the screen. "Will Mrs Hillier please go to the foyer." "That must be me," I said to my parents.

Outside I found my younger sister, June. "Hilda," she said, "you have to go to the police station. There's a phone message for you. It's from Norman. He's going to ring at 9.30."

My husband had been captured by the Japanese and held prisoner. I hadn't seen him for five years. When he phoned, he said he had just arrived at Southampton on the liner *Queen Elizabeth*. It was so wonderful to hear his voice again after all that time.

The next day he arrived home. Standing on the platform at Hull Paragon Station is a memory I shall never forget.' *(Hilda Hellier – Bempton WI)*

A Child's War

For those who were young, war soon became almost a natural part of life. Some children were evacuated away from the areas under greatest threat and faced a new life, others suffered through the air raids with their friends and family. Getting 'back to normal' when Daddy at last came home proved, often, as hard to cope with as the war itself had been.

▧ The Smell of Honeysuckle ▧

'When the war started I was nine years old. One day my friend and I were out on our bicycles when the air raid siren sounded, but before we could reach home two land mines were dropped by enemy aircraft in a nearby field. I don't think we have ever pedalled so fast in our lives.

Once a barrage balloon left its moorings in Hull, 20 miles away. They were put up to try and stop enemy aircraft flying over the city. This particular balloon narrowly missed my father and his horse in a field; the metal rope was dangling and would have sliced into the horse if it had been a few inches nearer.

My father made use of the balloon, which landed in a tree. It was a tough grey material. Out came Grandma's treadle sewing machine and Dad produced trousers for my brothers, shopping bags and even a stack sheet.

Our air raid shelter was underground, dug by my father and our neighbour. The beds were sacks filled with straw and lighting was with paraffin lamps. It was quite cosy once inside.

One happy memory is the smell of honeysuckle late at night as we ran down the lane to the shelter.

My father kept a lot of rabbits during the war. We were not allowed to "pet" them as they were part of our diet helping the rations along. The skins were cured, sometimes on the back of the door, spread out and treated with alum. Others were sent to Waddingtons in Hull and made into fur gloves. Our local doctor had a pair made with long gauntlets to keep him warm on cold winter days.' *(Jean Dowling – Hollym WI)*

▣ SOLDIERS EVERYWHERE ▣

'On 4th November 1939 I was in Sunday school along with all the other children, when suddenly we heard the sound of vehicles on the bottom street. We could hardly wait to see what was going on. We came out of church and went up to Top Street where we saw a soldier standing near the Concert Hall. I noticed his cap badge was a galloping horse, and in answer to our many questions he told us that 'B' Squadron, the 3rd King's Own Hussars had arrived in Londesborough. We dashed round the village and discovered trucks and tanks in the Stable Yard and Woodyard, and soldiers everywhere.

On Boxing Day the 3rd entertained all the children to a party in the Concert Hall, which by now had become the soldiers' mess room. When we came out after the party all the tanks were waiting outside to give us rides round the village. As it was 'B' Squadron, all the names of the tanks began with 'B' – Brown Jack, Bison, Belligerent etc. I rode in Brown Jack with Corporal Phil Jones driving. Phil Jones was billeted along with seven others in a bedroom up the back stairs at Warrendale Farm, so we got to know them very well.' *(Dulcie Huitson, of Market Weighton)*

▣ BOMBED OUT ▣

'In the 1940s I lived with my Mum and Dad in an ordinary semi in Driffield. We had two downstairs rooms, referred to as the living room and the "front room". This latter was a room used only for special events – Christmas, birthdays etc. It always smelled of soot. We didn't have heating except the fire, which was only lit on these special occasions. I was allowed the electric fire when I did my piano practice.

Towards the middle years of the Second World War our relations descended on us one by one as they were bombed out of Hull. My grandmother and grandfather who worked in Hull travelled daily from Driffield to Hull but came to live with us. Soon after, my aunt arrived and she became a clippie on the buses, coming and going at all hours. She was followed by her army husband and her son from Leeds. They all came to live in our semi – but only using the living room. Still the Front Room was kept special and the eight of us plus two evacuees all squashed into the one room. I still live in that semi.' *(Bunty Appleby – Nafferton WI)*

▨ EVACUATED ▨

'When the war came, four of the boys were evacuated but my mother would not let the two younger ones go unless I could go with them. As I went with schoolchildren, I too had to go back to school. We were taken by train to Scarborough on 1st September, each child being given a brown paper carrier bag with items of food in. I only remember two of them, perhaps because I liked these. One was corned beef and the other Nestlè's sweetened condensed milk. I sneaked a bit on my finger after dipping it in the open tin many a time.

We were taken to Northstead School and there we had to wait till someone came to take us to their home. Bob and Herbert went to Mrs C's on Tennyson Avenue, Frank and David and me went with Mrs D to Maple Drive. We were only there a week when they asked us if we could find somewhere else. I think they were too old to be bothered with children. We then went to Trafalgar Square to the home of Mr and Mrs A. Their house backed on to the cricket field. We had to go into the attic. You can imagine them not being very pleased as they would have been fully booked for the cricket season. By 25th September we had

I WISH TO MARK, BY THIS PERSONAL MESSAGE, my appreciation of the service you have rendered to your Country in 1939.

In the early days of the War you opened your door to strangers who were in need of shelter, & offered to share your home with them.

I know that to this unselfish task you have sacrificed much of your own comfort, & that it could not have been achieved without the loyal co-operation of all in your household.

By your sympathy you have earned the gratitude of those to whom you have shown hospitality, & by your readiness to serve you have helped the State in a work of great value.

The message sent to all those who took in evacuees during the war.
(Olive Middlewood – Kilham WI)

188

returned home.

We were back on Hedon Road in Hull before the blitz in May 1941, but we were lucky to survive among the rubble. We had an air raid shelter built by the Air Ministry as we backed on to woodyards by the side of Victoria Dock. We were considered to be in a danger area. Having nowhere now to eat and sleep, most of the family were taken by bus to Laxton village hall near Goole. There we slept on the floor or had chairs for the night, before being moved on to Saltmarsh Hall where we were given some stable rooms to stay in. I don't think we were there very long before we went to live in one of a pair of wooden bungalows between Paull and Thorngumbald. There we had a land mine dropped very close by, which caused the gable end to bend outwards, so it was not very safe!' *(Ruth Walker – Bishop Wilton WI)*

❖ Not a Great Life ❖

'During the summer before the war, the local Council came and made "dugout shelters" in all the gardens. They proved to be a complete waste of time and effort because the hole just filled up with water after rainfall and they were dangerous when small children played round them.

War was declared in 1939 and fear came into our lives. Real air raid shelters were built and lots of children were evacuated. My sister and I were among them. We were loaded into trains at Paragon station carrying a bag with a change of clothes, a toothbrush and a towel and with our gas masks in a box slung over our shoulders. Neither we nor our parents knew where we were headed for and we were waved off with tears and smiles from both children and mothers. We found ourselves in the Royal Hotel in Scarborough where we stayed for a few weeks. (Like lots of buildings the hotel had been commandeered by the Government.) We liked being by the sea but were terribly homesick for our parents and they decided that it would not be a safe place for us if the enemy decided to bombard the coast for any reason.

During the blitz on Hull, not only was my school demolished by fire bombs but our house was bomb damaged too on the same night. We had earlier moved back into the town to be nearer to my father's work. We moved into a Council house not far from where we used to live and so began our wartime experiences of blackouts, food rationing, the men all going off into the Forces and shortages of everything – not a great life for anyone and especially the teenagers.

I left school prematurely because of the demolition of the school and took a job. Overnight, I was expected to leave childhood behind and become a working adult with responsibilities. My mother had had my hair permed and she exchanged my short socks for stockings with an awful thing called a 'suspender belt'. I worked all the week for 12s 6d and later on when I joined the Education Department as a junior clerk I earned the princely sum of 16s 8d, which was promptly handed over to my mother who gave me 3s 6d back. It was winter when I started work. I cycled into the town or took a bus if the weather was snowy and we were in total blackout when I left at the end of the day. I certainly grew up quickly!' *(Joan Holt – Cottingham Green WI)*

▓ THE FUNNY GAME ▓

'My brother and I were evacuees based in Scarborough but in 1940 had come home to Hull for a few days. It was a warm summer's day and we decided to visit our favourite place, the cricket ground on Anlaby Road.

We ambled around and finally sat on the wooden seats, which were really like planks about a foot wide, around the ground. The grass had grown high and all we could hear were the birds and the distant sound of traffic. Then at the other side of the field a group of about a dozen men appeared. They carried broom handles, spades, forks and axes over their shoulders. Marching up and down they went, one man shouting orders what to do. Up, down, around they went, then suddenly they were flat on the ground, wriggling through the grass. We watched in amazement this funny game played by men.

Growing up we realised we had seen part of the birth of the Home Guard, or "Dad's Army" as it became affectionately called.' *(V. Osgerby – Cottingham WI)*

◙ Vivid Memories ◙

'My father was a painter and decorator – "time served" he would say, but there was very little work in Bridlington, consequently he joined the Royal Engineers at the start of the war. I think I must have been about four years of age when we moved to Dunswell. My grandmother had died and of course there was nothing for it as my mother being the youngest of six had to look after my grandad, who had unfortunately suffered a stroke shortly after retirement. He had worked for the Hull Telephone Company, as it was then called.

I have the most vivid memories of seeing Hull "on fire" – I believe that was when some of the worst bombing of the city took place. The sky was red with flames and we watched this awesome spectacle from the bedroom window.

Another event I will never forget, was when my mother and I took my grandfather for a walk. He was in his wheelchair and we pushed him down Dunswell Lane, when suddenly a plane flew low and fired. We had to jump in the dyke for cover – this was a really frightening experience.

I attended the village school and I can see even now the bottles of milk standing in their crates near the open fire warming, with a view to melting the ice which had formed. On reflection, we did seem to have some really bad winters and I have so many memories of sledding on Barmston Drain bank. One year in particular, the ice was so thick that practically the whole village skated on the drain – this would never be allowed now, as it is such a dangerous practice.

The dentist was an annual visitor to the school and I am sure that I speak for many people of my age, that we were instilled with a terrible fear of dentists for the rest of our lives. I can truthfully say that I have never met anyone so cruel as my childhood dentist.

There was very little entertainment, but some of the WI ladies formed a concert party and these shows were a great success. The village institute was always packed to capacity, in fact it was usually standing room only. We did have the occasional film show, also in the institute. I remember vividly that we would just be engrossed in the story and the reel would snap and the lights would be put on so that the film could be repaired.

My mother and aunt were stalwarts of the WI and for all there was a war on, I can still see them setting out for the meetings with bags full of sandwiches and cakes for refreshments – there did not seem to be much in the way of rationing at the meetings! Canning fruit – peaches and pears etc – was very much in vogue and proved to be a time consuming occupation for the ladies of the WI. My mother and aunt had a canning machine and the houses seemed to be constantly full of wasps and boiling coppers.' *(Jean Hammond – Leven WI)*

▩ Such a Lot to Answer For ▩

'I was born in July 1940, in my grandparents' home in Hull. The previous two nights, Hull had been bombed remorselessly, but on the night during which I was born, the German planes were silent.

My father, whose call-up had been deferred until after my birth, was despatched to fetch the midwife, who was apparently busy elsewhere. He was sent off to find another one, but by the time he returned the original midwife was there and it was all over, I had arrived.

For the first year of my life, most of my nights were spent sleeping in a washing basket in the air raid shelter.

My father was soon in the army, though stationed in England, and during my second year my mother was able to take me and go to live for six months in Melton Mowbray, close to where he was stationed. He was then moved elsewhere, and we returned to Hull, first to live with my grandparents, and then my mother obtained a Corporation house two doors away from them. My

Kilham's VJ Day celebrations, 3rd October 1945. (Isobel Shepherdson – Stamford Bridge WI)

father occasionally returned home on leave, but inevitably we did not see him very often, and contact was usually by letters and cards.

When I was a little older, my mother took a job, and I spent my days with Nana (Grandad was at work, too, of course), my uncle, twelve years older than me, who became my hero, and also my recently widowed aunt and two younger cousins.

Meanwhile, towards the end of the war my father was sent to Belgium, where he saw not one enemy aircraft. He tells me that throughout the whole of his war service, both in England and abroad, he felt he was safer than we were in Hull.

Later, the war having ended, my father returned home, a stranger – to me at least. My mother left her job, and my weekend treats ceased. Not so very long after that, my baby brother arrived. My life had changed completely, and it was all the fault of this stranger, my father.

Looking back, I realise that I was about twelve years old before I had a normal relationship with my father, and that our relationship was yet another of the casualties of World War Two. I also believe that we were not the only family who were affected in this way. War has such a lot to answer for!' *(Anon)*

▣ THE PRICE OF A BANANA ▣

'The husband of one of our members went to Goole station in 1943 to meet his sister who was married to a Maltese soldier. She had lived in Malta and had not been back to Goole since the outbreak of the war. She now had two small children and with great excitement he awaited the arrival of the train, with the long-lost members of the family, looking forward to seeing his sister and her children.

The train arrived and the party stepped off. Bags and luggage followed. Peter's eyes were riveted on the bag which had a big bunch of bananas on top. The eagerly awaited family was now forgotten as all he had eyes for were – the bananas!

His sister could see he was mesmerised – he hadn't seen one for four years, and she broke off a banana and handed it to Peter.

He carried it lovingly all the way home, quite oblivious of the chatting and catching up of four years of life. He put it beside him on the table at meal-times, took it to bed and it was there, the first thing to see, when he woke up the next morning.

It was a school day. He took the banana to school and basked in his fame of owning a banana. He finally ate it after his school lunch. It was beginning to deteriorate and had become decidedly spotted and tired-looking, so he decided he could not put off the bliss of eating it any longer. He was looked upon by many envious and open-mouthed school chums. But then he was offered a shining threepenny bit for the skin, which he promptly took, clinching the deal in seconds!' *(Brenda Kelly – Marshland WI)*

HIGHDAYS&HOLIDAYS

A YEAR OF CELEBRATION

The year had a rhythm of its own, studded with traditional events that made up our calendar, as one lady who grew up in Cottingham in the 1920s recalls.

'The year's events when I was a child from 1921 went something like this:

January – New Year's Tea at Sunday school in the school room, King Street. Usual games – Farmer wants a wife, Postman's Knock, Forfeits, etc.

January 1 – Lucky Bod first footing, my father (dark man) brought in coal and wood.

February 2 – Candlemas Day –
    'If Candlemas be fair and bright
    Winter will have another flight
    But if it be dark with clouds and rain
    Winter is gone and won't come again'.

April 1 – All Fools Day until 12 o'clock. Usual jokes, 1d worth of pigeon's milk etc. If anyone tried to do an April Fool after noon the rhyme was chanted, 'April Fool Day's past and gone, you're a fool for making one'. Afternoon was Legging Down Day, excuse for rough play by the boys!

Mothering Sunday – Violets or primroses for your mother – no cards.

Easter – Pancakes on Shrove Tuesday. Good Friday – fish bought from hawker with a barrow. Hot cross buns and Easter eggs. Good Friday – local boys walked up to the chalk pits near Skidby, gangs of boys walked from Hull also. They took boiled eggs, hot cross buns and a potato. I can remember seeing the boys walking down Northgate on a Good Friday before the war. Easter Sunday, had to wear something new, or the birds

A steam engine provides the pulling power for this outing in the early 1900s. (Isobel Shepherdson – Stamford Bridge WI)

would soil your clothes!

May – The last Sunday in May was the Primitive Methodist Sunday school anniversary. (The Wesleyans' was the first Sunday in June.) Special hymns and recitations by children. Girls had new dresses and many boys had lily of the valley buttonholes. Three services on Sunday, and one on the following Monday evening. No applause was given on the Sunday but allowed on the Monday night service, and the poems were of a less religious nature.

May 24 – Empire Day at school. We wore daisies, symbol of the mother country and the Empire. Our headmistress was a very patriotic lady.

May – Chapel School Feast – Wednesday following the anniversary, had a party similar to the one held at the New Year, but if it was fine we had sports in a farmer's field after tea in the school-room.

Whitsuntide – Flowers taken to school to be sold for charity – think it was in aid of Sailors' Orphans Homes in Hull. Some

Great fun – a winkle competition at Spurn Point c1900. (East Riding of Yorkshire Council, Library and Information Services)

years flowers were difficult to find.

July 15 – St Swithin's Day – rain on this day and it would rain for 40 days.

July – Cottingham Flower Show – held in a marquee in the grounds of some of the large houses, eg Westfield. I remember a concert party in another marquee at the same place in the evening.

July – Club Feast. Fair held on the market green – remnants of the Club feasts held by the Free Gardeners Club in Cottingham. Roundabouts, stalls, dodgems, etc but in earlier times stalls had been erected in the streets.

July – Last Wednesday – Sunday school trip to Bridlington. The chapels (four) hired a train to Bridlington for parents and children. Cottingham village practically empty of people on this day. My father didn't go on the trip and usually white-washed the outside of the cottage while we were away.

August – Bank Holiday Monday – Cottingham Horse Show, held in different locations in the village. Classes for cows (my father

On the sands at Bridlington in the 1920s.
(Shirley Franklin – Driffield WI)

won two cups in 1928), horses, ponies, show-jumping and horse-racing in the evening. The decorated shire horses were magnificent. Displays of the Holderness fox-hounds and sheep dog demonstrations etc. Cottingham Silver Band played selections of music in the afternoon and various marquees were erected.

Harvest – Harvest festival at the chapels. Sale of produce for chapel funds.

Oct. 12 – Hull Fair. We always visited Bostock & Wombwell's menagerie – I took a bag of fallen apples to give to the animals, and I remember a ride on an elephant! Remember the flea circus, wall of death, cakewalk, gallopers etc. Had peas and chips in 'Carvers' tent and went home with brandy snap, nougat and a 'cupie' celluloid dolly.

Oct 31/Nov 4 – Did not celebrate either Halloween or Mischief night as far as I recall.

Nov. 5 – Bonfire Night – many communal bonfires in village on every spare piece of land in Cottingham including the Market

Green and West Green.

Nov. 11 – Armistice Day celebrated at school with patriotic service and 2 minute silence kept at 11 am.

'If there's ice in November to carry a duck
There'll be nothing after but sludge and muck'

December – Christmas – preparations didn't start so early pre-war as they do now. The first thing to start the Christmas season when I was a child was the arrival of the local grocer's shop travellers with a case of samples of Christmas 'goodies', fancy boxes of biscuits, bottles of boiled sweets, chocolates, etc, and touting for orders. Christmas pudding mixture was stirred and a wish made, silver sixpences and threepenny 'dodgers' put in the mixture for luck. Christmas puddings, cakes and mincemeat were prepared and sometimes we killed a pig. My grandad came for a week before Christmas to help with our ducks and cockerels which were 'dressed and drawn' for orders. We always hoped for cold weather in the week or ten days before Christmas as there was no refrigerator.

I made a 'mistletoe' with two hoops to make a sort of garland, decorated with frills of cut tissue paper of different colours. This was hung with baubles, sugar mice, bird cages and bundles of chocs in coloured silver paper and a Japanese lantern was placed in the centre of the mistletoe. We decorated pictures and clocks with holly, but had no tree. All decorations were taken down before Twelfth Night as it was unlucky to leave them up afterwards.

Small girls went round neighbours' houses 'vessel cupping'. They asked for a penny to see the dolly in the shoe box. Carol singers went round the houses and also Cottingham Band and the Salvation Army playing carols.

Not so many Christmas cards were sent, there was a post on Christmas morning. Advertising calendars were given by grocers, millers etc to their customers for Christmas presents.

Dec. 24 – Frummety night – Christmas Eve. We were given a small parcel of 'pearled' wheat by the miller at Skidby Mill. My mother 'creed' it in a brown pot in the side oven, then it was boiled with milk like porridge and served with sugar, cream, rum etc and eaten at supper-time. If the sun shone through the apple trees on Christmas Day there would be a good crop of apples the next year.' *(Eileen Green – Cottingham WI)*

---·---

SUMMER DELIGHTS

---·---

*D*ays *on the beach, new clothes at Whitsuntide, May Day, Feasts and Walks all brightened the summer days. And there were Royal summers too, when we all joined in the celebrations for coronations or jubilees.*

▨ NEW CLOTHES AT WHITSUNTIDE ▨

'It was traditional on Whit Monday to go to Grandma's and show her my new clothes. Nearly all children got some, if not all, new clothes at Whitsuntide.

Cycling was a popular pastime in the 1930s – this cycling club was preparing for a chilly Bank Holiday ride to the coast.

At South Cave Carnival, 1911 – some of the workers! (East Riding of Yorkshire Council, Library and Information Services)

My cousins and I were all taken off to Grandma's house in the morning, and on arrival we paraded and twirled before her and Auntie V. Afterwards we were summoned to Grandma's side for inspection, and the first thing she did was to lift up the hem of our dresses to see what we were wearing underneath. Every year she said the same thing: "I'll not have penny tops and farthing bottoms!" After her approval we then changed into our older clothes and after dinner we were taken to the annual fair, complete with a whole sixpence from Grandma. My cousins had a great time on the roundabouts but I never liked them so I spent my money on the lovely sticky curled brandy snap that was always made at the fair.' *(H.M. Garner – Atwick WI)*

▨ MAY DAY AT BISHOP WILTON ▨

'In the 1930s Bishop Wilton Church of England school celebrated May Day in style. Mr and Mrs Rhodes, the headmaster and his wife, introduced the Crowning of the May Queen. The pupils,

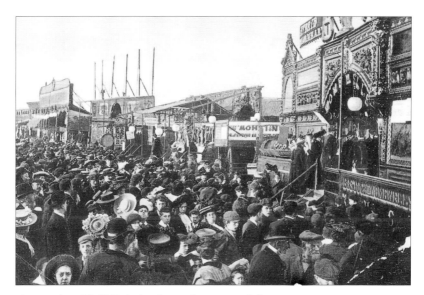

A crowd at Hull Fair in the early years of the century. (East Riding of Yorkshire Council, Library and Information Services)

their ages ranging from five to 14, voted for the girl they thought most suited to be their Queen, and the runners up were attendants.

The May Queen then decided on a flower name. I have happy memories of being chosen in 1936, and using the unusual title of Queen Arabis after the little white rockery flowers in bloom in a nearby cottage garden.

On the day the Queen and attendants wore pretty white dresses, and the crowning ceremony was done by a local lady interested in the school or the retiring Queen, who wore a plainer coronet while handing over the glittering zig-zag style crown to the lucky new holder of the title. A local dignitary (sometimes the Countess of Halifax) attended with many parents and village folk, who all enjoyed the maypole and other country dances, especially the favourite "Rufty Tufty". After the entertainment refreshments were served and the Queen received a small gift as a memento. The school had at that time two beautifully carved oak boards on which the names of May Queens and School

Captains were recorded in gold lettering, made by a local joiner, Mr Walker, father of the first May Queen Barbara (Queen Wallflower).' *(Lorna Sleightholme – Bishop Wilton WI)*

▣ EMPIRE DAY ▣

'The highlight of our year was Empire Day, when the school hall became a theatre. I was eight years old when I was chosen to be Britannia. I wore a white tunic and a golden helmet, and carried a trident and a Union Jack shield. I had to say: "I am Mother Britannia, my birthday is today, boys and girls remember the 24th May."

Mothers and fathers were there to see each boy or girl walk in turn down the aisle to Britannia. They were dressed in costumes of every country in the Empire and carried gifts. Each one presented their gift, then laid it on the floor and was thanked. One by one they gathered round my chair in a colourful group. Then we sang *Rule Britannia*, helped by teachers and parents.

We were not so respectful out in the playground. The year was 1936 and we were aware of the news and gossip about the King, who later abdicated in December. We walked round singing:

Who's that coming down the street?
Mrs Simpson in her bare feet.
Who's that knocking on Edward's door?
She's been married twice before…Yah, Yah…Yah, Yah!'

(Jessie Freeman – Driffield WI)

▣ ROYAL SUMMERS ▣

'In 1935, the year of George V's Silver Jubilee, the King and Queen were due to come through our village one evening on their celebration tour. I was seven at the time. My father took me and my elder brother and little sister up to the village green to see them pass. We waited a long time and people said they were late. Suddenly a loud cheer went up, followed by laughter. My father picked up my sister and me to see over the heads of the crowd. Then a little Austin Seven came slowly down the hill. I

Competitors at Driffield's 1935 Jubilee celebrations. (Mrs Minns – Driffield WI)

was rather surprised at the King and Queen travelling in an Austin Seven since we had a Morris Ten, but we peered into the little car and cheered and waved like everyone else.

Next morning in assembly the headmistress read out a letter. The King was very sorry but he had been so tired after his visit to Birmingham that he had proceeded straight to Chatsworth for the night. He knew all the children would have been very disappointed so he had asked Messrs Cadbury to supply them all with a half-pound block of Dairy Milk Chocolate. (The boys at the school next door only got one bar between two!) So, I had seen the King and Queen – or as good as – and received a huge bar of chocolate as well.' *(Freda Feaster – Howden WI)*

'The highlight of 1937 was the Coronation. There was a service in Londesborough church and then sports and teas in the Pleasure Grounds. I had been practising running for days and I was delighted when I won a prize. All the prizes had been donated by Mrs Booth, and they were displayed on a table under the yew trees. The races were run down the broad walk in the

A Coronation souvenir programme for 1937. (Joan Holt – Cottingham Green WI)

Wilderness and the finishing tape was in the Pleasure Grounds. Uncle Herbert was responsible for getting the runners lined up and his megaphoned voice could be heard all over the grounds: "Any more for any more?"

There were very few cars in the village at that time, so it was a great novelty that afternoon when Mr Kitching from the post office brought his car down to the grounds so that everyone could listen to the King's speech. Mr Kitching's car was the only one in the village to be equipped with a radio, or a wireless set as we called it in those days. After the service Mrs Booth planted two chestnut trees to mark the event, having planted two trees two years before to mark the Jubilee.' *(Dulcie Huitson, of Market Weighton)*

'After the hard post-war years, happier times came in 1953. The Queen's Coronation was watched by many, crowded into sitting rooms to share the television viewing on the few nine-inch screens. Some people actually had twelve-inch sets! And then the parties everywhere. Fangfoss with Bolton's Coronation Celebration programme began the night before with a dance in the school. On the day itself, 3rd June, there was a children's fancy dress parade followed by children's sports, and then souvenirs were distributed to them all as they left school after the tea. In the afternoon there was a comic cricket match and adult sports – which included Throwing the Cricket Ball, Horse and Jockey, Slow Bicycle Race, and Married Women's Races. All followed by a Social – and cries of "God Save the Queen"!' *(Ella Musgrove for Fangfoss with Bolton WI)*

▣ Middleton Feast ▣

'The anniversary of the Middleton-on-the-Wolds Foresters which took place annually on the second Friday in June, was known locally as Middleton Feast.

The Foresters was a society formed to help working men, who paid a subscription to give them a little security when sick or to help their families with funeral expenses. All the members had to be of good character and behaviour. On the Friday previous to the anniversary parade all members had to attend the court, as it was called, in the Robin Hood pub where they had a special room.

The eight officers elected were in charge of the court. I can remember my father going to this meeting armed with Mansion Polish and dusters to clean the banner. Dad was very tall which made him an ideal standard bearer.

The Thursday before the parade the fun fair came to the village. I remember in 1935, excitement grew in the school playground. We knew roughly the time they came, as it was usually in the afternoon play time. The cry would go up, "Corrigans are coming". We all ran to the bottom gate just in time. We could hear the rumble of the massive steam engine, the large wheels clattering along. All eyes looked to the right just in time to see the black smoke belching, the black canopy over the engine nosing over the hill top, the gleaming brass poles glinting in the sun at the front of this monster. We cheered and shouted as it passed in a few minutes, pulling the coal tender followed by beautifully painted caravans with pretty lace curtains, the water cart and the stalls and rides stacked on the trailers.

The school bell called us back to lessons until 3.30 pm. After tea we were allowed to go to the fairground until eight o'clock. How we enjoyed just sitting on the grass watching the men erecting the roundabouts and side-shows. How hard they worked with their skilful hands covered in grease, strong muscular arms and fleet of foot. All had a cosmopolitan look about them. The church clock struck eight, time to go home. Tomorrow would be a great day.

Friday morning, brilliant sunshine, with excitement growing we washed the pots and fetched the milk from the farm. We put on new dresses, socks and shoes. Mother tied our hair with a white ribbon – mine always slipped off. All the Foresters assembled at the tradesmen's entrance of the rectory, the officers with their sashes and stars, the others in flat caps and boots. Driffield Silver Band was in attendance.

The parade began. First the standard, large and green, proudly

The Middleton Foresters parade. (Marie Grice – Bainton WI)

held aloft, flanked by the officers and followed by the band playing loudly. Bringing up the rear were the younger members carrying the staves. How proud they were. All the village turned out to cheer them as they moved up the village, round the top end and back down Back Street and round to the church again.

They all trooped into the church and so did we. The service seemed endless. I got the fidgets and a slap. After the service the men marched to a nearby field to a marquee for lunch which they had to pay a shilling for. The Robin Hood prepared the food – roast beef and feast plum pudding with a glass of beer. After lunch the local dignitaries gave speeches and the Foresters their reports.

We had to change our dresses and shoes. How I loved my cotton flowered dress and sandals – sheer freedom. After tea we were given 3d to spend at the fair, so off we went. At the field entrance was a sweet stall with a sloping counter beautifully stacked with crisp curly brandy snap, neat white packets of

Doncaster butterscotch, liquorice bootlaces, sherbet dabs, pink sugar pigs, Smith's crisps with the blue twist of salt and every sweet you could think of. We looked and walked on. Close by a delicious smell, small dishes of hot peas and mint sauce 6d each. We couldn't afford them so on we went to a small roundabout for the under fives. We watched the lean lady in the brown coat turning the large iron wheel by hand, how clever she was at regulating the speed. We were told to ride on that. The brightly painted swing boats swinging high and low, these made Joyce feel sick so we moved on.

Rolling pennies, I was sure I would win – no luck. My penny rolled and dropped on the line. Coconut shies with coconuts securely perched on stilts like cups were too difficult for us to dislodge. The darts, dozens of playing cards pinned on boards, hit three for a prize. We decided against it. The shooting range with prizes galore, toys, vases, soft dolls, all looked brilliant under bright lights; young men were hitting targets and bullseyes, but not for us. The hoopla stall, it looked easy, prizes sat on wooden blocks, the ring must go over the block, mine didn't! I had 1d left and I knew how I wanted to spend it. The speedway was what I longed for, the blue and red steps up to the platform, brightly painted animals and motor bikes with a safety rail securely bolted on to the moving floor. The music played, the lights flashed, I chose a motor bike to ride on, hold tight and off we go.

The men collected the money while the speedway was in motion. They seemed to glide around keeping their balance, and how smart and dashing they looked with their curly Brylcremed hair. Round and round we went, hair flying. I had to cling to the rails. Gradually it slowed and stopped – it was great. My 3d spent, I went to find Mother and Aunt Alice. We watched the throng until it was dark and then went home to bed.

Saturday morning bright sunshine again. We did the usual chores and in the afternoon we went to the field with another 3d. I had three rides in the afternoon because it was 2d a ride in the evening. Dad came to the fair in the evening. He took me for a last ride on the speedway and I was delighted – sheer joy.

Sunday we went to the field – everything had gone. The end of a lovely weekend. Then in 1939 the war came and there were no more parades or funfairs.' *(Marie Grice – Bainton WI)*

▨ KILHAM CLUB FEAST AND ANNUAL TRIP ▨

'I was born in Kilham in 1909. Kilham Club Feast was always on the last Wednesday in June and it was a school holiday. Corrigans set up the stalls, swingboats, coconut shy, roll a penny, sweet stalls etc on the Tuesday. There was always "The Fattest Woman" and a bearded lady, and a hand-worked roundabout for small children. This took place in the field corner opposite the school.

The Club Feast started off with Driffield Silver Band and the parade of the Foresters. Tommy Scott and Brian Milner led the Foresters, dressed in green, wearing tricorn hats and carrying a large bow and arrow each about 6 foot tall. The rest of the Foresters were dressed in green and had green bandeaux on their hats. They paraded from Pasture Gate Farm to the parish church where they had a service, then on to the Temperance Hall for

All set for the Kilham Village Trip. (Cecily Wilson – Kilham WI)

The annual outing from the Ship Inn, Dunswell in the 1950s.
(J. Wilson – Kilham WI)

dinner of roast beef, new potatoes, green peas, plum pudding and rum sauce. The joints were cooked at the homes of Mr Tommy Frost and Butcher Robinson.

Everyone went to the fair and also races in Wilson's field on Millside. Then there was a dance at the Temperance Hall.

Kilham Annual Trip took place on a Wednesday and was governed by the time of the tides. All the local farmers supplied horses and waggons to take the schoolchildren and their mothers to Bridlington; this was a highlight of the year and it was the only time that some saw the sea. Everyone was dressed in their best clothes and the waggons were clean and the horses beautifully decorated with horse brasses. There was also a clean canvas cover in case of rain and the taller passengers had to be at each corner to hold up the canvas. My husband remembered when waggoner and wags used to sit up the night before the trip so that the horses didn't lie down and spoil the decorations.

The families enjoyed the beach and when they returned to the village about 7 or 8 pm everyone turned out to welcome them home.' *(Cecily Wilson – Kilham WI)*

CHRISTMAS PAST

T he scents and sounds of Christmas were very special, often enhanced by traditions that we all enjoyed.

▨ CHRISTMAS AT BUTTERCRAMBE ▨

'At Christmas time we used to do all the poultry and get that ready for sale but we never did a lot of shopping for Christmas until Christmas Eve, when Dad used to go into York and do the shopping. We only bought Christmas presents for the family and it was only the youngest who used to hang their stockings up. When you got to a certain age, that was it and you were off the list. It certainly wasn't the performance that it is now – if you sent Christmas cards, you could post them on Christmas Eve and the recipient would probably get them on Christmas Day.

Of the toys which I remember getting, though these were very few, as a child I can remember getting a succession of dolls. These disappointed me, because in a very short time they had become bald. Their lovely curly tresses were just stuck on and soon came off. My Aunt Carrie had made a couple of dolls for her daughter and made their 'hair' out of sheep's wool. I spent hours brushing, combing and plaiting the doll's hair during visits there – and it didn't come off!

One year for Christmas I got a doll's pram. One year we all got a fancy decorated mug and the three youngest of us got a cup and saucer. There wasn't usually much more than one piece and your stocking. The contents of the stocking were very traditional;

a piece of coal, a few nuts, an apple, an orange, a few sweets and a chocolate or pink fondant mouse or perhaps a chocolate Father Christmas. Perhaps there might be a little book or a paintbox or something simple in there as well.

For decoration we used to have a tree which would probably have come from the hedgerow. There were so many glass baubles which used to come out year after year and a few paper streamers, and then if we were a bit short we used to put on our beads and old shiny jewellery. There were candles too, some on little clips. We didn't light these very often so they lasted a number of years. Elsewhere in the house we always had some holly in, over the mantlepiece and the mirror and maybe a sprig or two of mistletoe.

Mother used to be baking right up to supper time on Christmas Eve, icing the cake and whatever and then we always had 'frummerty'. Originally it was a kind of wheat which you used to stew and stew and stew in the oven and then slop some sultanas and sugar in it. Latterly we used to have a sort of Quaker Oats and call that frummerty.

We usually had goose on Christmas Day and probably a lump of pork, together with various vegetables and stuffings, followed by Christmas pudding and rum sauce. We would get cracking with the cooking at about 9 am doing the potatoes and sprouts. Some of the cooking was done on the old range and some of the vegetable pans would be done on the open fire on a grid iron thing. We would have a meal, about up to 'the top notch', and then we would sit around and Mother would bring out some of her sweeties. She used to buy some of these pink fondants with hazelnuts, hazelnut creams and some special biscuits. I thought they were gorgeous and we would sit in the afternoon and chew away. Dad loved nuts and he would buy about a stone at a time. He would sit there with his nutcrackers, chewing until you would think he would spoil his innards for ever more. Teatime, we would probably have cheese and celery, trifle and umpteen cakes and pastries. A piece of coffee cake, a piece of orange cake, a macaroon, some mince pies; you reckoned to go around the lot – I don't know how we ate it!

In the evening we often had someone playing the piano and singing carols. Other entertainments were cards and dominoes or perhaps we might do a bit of dancing in the kitchen. There was never a lot of drink. Christmas was a time when you would have a bottle of port and perhaps a bottle of whisky for the men, though it wasn't the family who drank it. Anyone who called over the Christmas period would get a piece of Christmas cake, a lump of cheese and a glass of port. It was always cake and cheese. In those early days we didn't even have the cake iced – it would have almonds on the top of a rich fruit cake. When we were younger George and I used to go out on Christmas Day to the next farm for a Christmas box and chant Christmas carols or such like:

"We wish you a merry Christmas
And a happy New Year
All good luck and all good cheer
Please can I be the lucky bird here?"

We would be invited in and given a piece of Christmas cake and 6d to go home with and that was our Christmas Feasting. Hubert and some of his merry men used to go Christmas singing. He would take his violin and four of them would sing part songs.

On Boxing Day we would eat up the cold meats and generally laze about. I used to like Boxing Day better than Christmas Day – that was too hectic! It was all hard work and cooking. On Boxing Day there was a dance down the village or round about which we would go to.' *(Daisy Naylor – Stamford Bridge WI)*

❊ Early Birds at Boynton ❊

'As a little girl I was brought up in the village of Boynton. On the kitchen window sill my Aunt Nellie always kept a small pot, in which she kept some small change, halfpennies, pennies and threepenny bits. Especially at Christmas time. Nothing unusual about that you may think.

On Christmas morning we always listened for a knock on the door, and listened very hard.

217

"I wish you a Merry Christmas and a Happy New Year
Good luck to you and all you have for next year.

A little bit of spice bread, a little bit of cheese
A cup of cold water and a penny if you please.

If you haven't got a penny then a halfpenny will do
If you haven't got a halfpenny – God Bless You."

What is this rhyme? you may ask. Well this was chanted by the Early Bird, whoever could be the earliest to knock on your door and say this rhyme. You were lucky if you got the full rhyme, usually only the first part was said. The Early Birds were always children, from the very young to those in their teens.

Now you will see why my aunt always had a pot of change handy. The Earliest Bird got the most, any after that got a little something. My father often used to tell me this tale. As a boy, he was an Early Bird himself.' *(B. Scrivener – Kilham WI)*

▨ A CHRISTMAS TREAT ▨

'More than 70 years ago, the children of Bainton school were given a small treat at Christmas time. The local Squire and his wife lived in Meswick Hall about one mile from the village. Most of the village properties belonged to the Meswick estate.

The children were pupils at the village school until they were 14 years old. Before the school closed for the Christmas holidays the Squire's wife arrived in a horse-drawn carriage at the village school. All the pupils had to be on their best behaviour. From her baskets the lady of the hall gave each child one mince pie, one apple, one silver sixpence. Imagine having 6d to spend.

Those were the days.' *(Marie Grice – Bainton WI)*

INDEX